THE LAST PLANTATION

The Last Plantation

RACISM AND RESISTANCE
IN THE HALLS OF CONGRESS

James R. Jones

PRINCETON UNIVERSITY PRESS
PRINCETON & OXFORD

Published by Princeton University Press
41 William Street, Princeton, New Jersey 08540
99 Banbury Road, Oxford OX2 6JX

press.princeton.edu

Library of Congress Cataloging-in-Publication Data

Names: Jones, James R., 1987- author.
Title: The last plantation : racism and resistance in the halls of Congress /
    James R. Jones.
Description: Princeton : Princeton University Press, 2024. | Includes
    bibliographical references and index.
Identifiers: LCCN 2023038429 (print) | LCCN 2023038430 (ebook) |
    ISBN 9780691223636 (hardback) | ISBN 9780691223643 (ebook)
Subjects: LCSH: United States. Congress—Officials and employees. |
    United States. Congress—Officials and employees—Legal status, laws, etc. |
    African American legislative employees. | Service industries workers—
    United States. | Racism in the workplace—United States. | Employee rights—
    United States. | BISAC: SOCIAL SCIENCE / Ethnic Studies / American /
    African American & Black Studies | SOCIAL SCIENCE / Race &
    Ethnic Relations
Classification: LCC JK1083 .J66 2024 (print) | LCC JK1083 (ebook) |
    DDC 328.73008996073—dc23/eng/20231102
LC record available at https://lccn.loc.gov/2023038429
LC ebook record available at https://lccn.loc.gov/2023038430

British Library Cataloging-in-Publication Data is available

Editorial: Meagan Levinson and Erik Beranek
Production Editorial: Ali Parrington
Jacket Design: Chris Ferrante
Production: Erin Suydam
Publicity: Alyssa Sanford and Kathryn Stevens
Copyeditor: Leah Caldwell

Jacket image: Leontura / iStock

This book has been composed in Miller

Printed in the United States of America

10 9 8 7 6 5 4 3 2 1

To the Black women who raised me,
taught me, and prayed for me.

And to the Black woman who did all the above,
my mom, Marian Roxanne Johnson.

CONTENTS

ACKNOWLEDGMENTS

IF YOU'RE READING this, it means that I have completed this book, a feat that I once thought was impossible. This project has been the most challenging task I've undertaken so far, spanning over thirteen years. Countless individuals have played a pivotal role in helping me bring this work to fruition. To my village, who uplifted and encouraged me, challenged me to be more precise and clearer, and instilled in me the confidence to trust my own instincts and intellect, I offer my heartfelt gratitude.

This book would not have happened without the support and mentorship of my old congressional office. My immense gratitude to Elizabeth King, Maisha Leek, Debra Anderson, Michelle Anderson Lee, Nuku Ofori, Brenden Chainey, and, of course, former Congressman Chaka Fattah. Furthermore, I am profoundly grateful to everyone I interviewed. I appreciate the time you spent with me and your honest reflections about life on Capitol Hill.

Embarking on this project as a doctoral student in sociology at Columbia University, I was privileged to receive the guidance and mentorship of an exceptional community of scholars. I feel incredibly fortunate to have had Alondra Nelson as my advisor, as she exemplified the highest standards of professionalism and academic rigor while remaining dedicated to social justice. I have such fond memories of our first meeting. I walked into her office carrying a small whiteboard, on which I had sketched out the early stages of my dissertation project. Overflowing with enthusiasm, she immediately picked up a dry-erase marker and added an "a" under the "o" in "Black Capitol," the title of my dissertation. Her encouragement to think deeply about the agency and power held by Black staffers has stayed with me ever since. Since that first meeting, she has remained a steadfast source of support and encouragement.

Diane Vaughan played an instrumental role in guiding this project from its inception. Through her scholarship and teaching, I acquired the tools to analyze Congress as a complex organization. Her enthusiastic feedback and constructive criticism were invaluable in shaping multiple drafts of my work. Tom DiPrete has also been a valuable mentor, providing unwavering support and encouraging me to apply my skills to quantitatively study Congress. Shamus Khan helped build my confidence as a young sociologist, always making time to respond to my emails, meet with me, and offer feedback that affirmed the value of my work. Last but not least, I am deeply grateful to Fred Harris, whose expertise in Black politics has been instrumental in grounding my work in a robust interdisciplinary framework.

I am immensely grateful for the guidance and mentorship provided by numerous esteemed faculty members throughout my doctoral program. Their unwavering support has not only shaped the contours of this project but has also played an instrumental role in my personal and professional growth as a scholar. I extend my heartfelt thanks to Van Tran, Fred Wherry, Gil Eyal, Sudhir Venkatesh, Josh Whitford, Peter Bearman, Mitch Duneier, Herbert Gans, Kimberley Johnson, Valerie Purdie Vaughans, and Mignon Moore. A special thank you to Carla Shedd, who encouraged me after my first semester to start my fieldwork immediately. Finally, I would also like to express my deep appreciation for the invaluable assistance provided by Afton Battle, Anne Born, Kiamesha Wilson, Dora Arenas, and the late Nusaiba Jackson.

I am grateful for the unparalleled teaching and advising that I received during my time as an undergraduate student at the George Washington University, which contributed to my success.

AAAA

I would like to extend my heartfelt appreciation to the exceptional faculty members, including Daina Eglitis, Derek Hyra, Adele Alexander, Steve Tuch, Greg Squires, and Sarah Binder.

Rutgers University-Newark was an enriching space to complete this manuscript, which reflects the visionary leadership of Chancellor Nancy Cantor and Dean Jacqueline Mattis. I would like to thank Zahra Ali, Elise Boddie, Sherri-Ann Butterfield, Melissa Cooper, Chris Duncan, Belinda Edmondson, Frank Edwards, Peter Englot, Alex Hinton, Peter Hepburn, Wendell Holbrook, Lacey Hunter, Jyl Josephson, John Keene, Wendell Marsh, Hyacinth Miller, Domingo Morel, Charles Payne, Mara Sidney, Timothy Stewart Winter, Salamishah Tillet, and Melissa Valle. I thank Corey Clawson, Rabeya Rahman, and Mi Hyun Yoon for their administrative assistance. A special thank you to Christina Strasburger for her heartfelt work to uplift faculty, students, and the Rutgers-Newark community. Lastly, I thank my research assistants Parmeda Abdollahnejad, Kai Cobbs, Jamie Larson, Arianna Reid Hill, Mireia Triguero Roura, Sherish Taqweem, and Tiffany Win.

Throughout my book-writing journey, I have found tremendous inspiration and support as an active member of both the Association for Black Sociologists and the National Conference for Black Political Scientists. These scholarly organizations have played a pivotal role in shaping my professional growth and fostering my adoption of critical race perspectives. Within these transformative spaces, I have had the privilege of connecting with exceptional colleagues and forging lasting friendships. I extend my gratitude to Littisha Bates, Nadia Brown, Derrick Brooms, Corey Fields, Saida Grundy, Amaka Okechukwu, Ravi Perry, Regina Dixon Reeves, Zandria Robinson, and BarBara Scott. In addition, I would like to express my deepest appreciation to Christina Greer. During my most challenging moments as a writer, she emerged as a radiant beacon of joy and hope. She also gifted me a magical hoodie that became a symbol of confidence and empowerment in my writing journey.

My research was supported by numerous fellowships and grants. Data for the book were collected while I was a graduate student at Columbia and National Science Foundation Research Fellow (Grant No. ANWER: DGE-07-07425). Additionally, while there I received a grant from the Dirksen Congressional Center. Next, I benefited immensely as a fellow in the Summer Institute on Tenure and Professional Advancement at Duke University. Through this program, I was mentored by Valeria Sinclair Chapman. We spoke twice a month for over two years, well beyond the official end of my fellowship. Valeria helped me transform my dissertation into a workable book manuscript with patience, compassion, and humor. Then, I was a postdoctoral fellow in the Department of African American Studies at Princeton University. Eddie Glaude and Keeanga-Yamahtta Taylor were amazing mentors who encouraged me to think boldly and swing big in my work. I also thank April Peters and Dionne Worthy for their administrative assistance. The department generously sponsored a manuscript workshop, and I am appreciative of Donald Tomaskovic-Devey and David Canon, who participated and offered incisive feedback. Lastly, the Rutgers' Institute for the Study of Global Racial Justice provided me with much-needed time to complete this manuscript and to do so in community with other racial justice scholars across Rutgers campuses. I am especially appreciative to Michelle Stephens, the institute's founding director, for her unwavering support and guidance.

I am deeply grateful for the exceptional team at Princeton University Press. Meagan Levinson, my editor, has been a remarkable source of support since the inception of this project. She expertly guided me through the production process and provided invaluable feedback that improved the book's quality. I also thank Erik Beranek, Ali Parrington, and Leah Caldwell for their assistance in the production process. The anonymous readers of my book proposal and manuscript offered insightful comments that strengthened the book's arguments. I also extend my heartfelt appreciation to Christie Henry, director of PUP, for her generosity in providing me with a grant that enabled me to cover the expenses for a coworking space, where I could focus on finishing my manuscript.

I cannot overstate the gratitude I feel toward David Lobenstine, whose expert guidance has helped me to refine my ideas, strengthen my arguments, and become a more confident writer. Equally instrumental in my book-writing journey has been Megan Close, who helped me navigate the challenges and complexities of being a first-time author. I am immensely grateful to Daniel Schuman, whose work I deeply admire, for generously reading portions of this manuscript and providing critical advice that was instrumental in completing this book.

I was fortunate to write this book in community with my closest friends, who were also completing their own book manuscripts. They are brilliant and beautiful writers, whom I continuously learn from. Catherine Tan and Heba Gowayed generously read multiple drafts, offered incisive feedback, and, most importantly, provided endless encouragement. It is hard to put into words what you two mean to me and the positive impact you have had on me intellectually and personally. My sincere apologies to your husbands, Joshua Tan and Nick Occhiuto, for stealing so much of your time the last few years, although this theft will continue. When I joined Rutgers-Newark, I had no idea I would gain both a brilliant colleague and close friend like Janice Gallagher, who constantly checked in on my well-being and motivated me across the finish line. In my final year of writing and revising, Andy McDowell was a constant and reassuring guide who helped me find my way through the thick fog that develops during the end of a long-term project.

I am grateful beyond measure to my friends outside of academia, whose unwavering support kept me grounded and provided a much-needed balance. Among them, Nisha Ramachandran, Kelly Kit, and Walter Scott-Williams hold a special place in my heart as friends who I have known for more than half of my life. Their steadfast presence has been an invaluable source of strength and sanity throughout my journey. I extend my thanks to Brian Ackerman, David Baiz, Desiree Barnes, Evon Burton, Tiffani Donaldson Berry, Keith Boykin, Shanise Bland, Rohit Chopra, Kenyon Farrow, Michael Fattica, Aja Gilliam, Morgan James, Sandeep and Semanti Kulkarni, Jessica Lau, Maisha Leek, Colin Lieu, Leyla Lindsay, Brian Pierce, Jason Resendez, Michael Rochon, Joe Scattergood, Julian Shanks, Ari Shaw, Arniece Stevenson, Newaye Tedla, Carlos Vera, and Heather Wilson.

My family cheered me on and were a source of inspiration throughout this process. I am deeply grateful to my aunts Carol Johnson and Kathy Jones, as well as my uncles Ronald Johnson and the late David Johnson, for their continuous support and guidance throughout my educational journey. I owe so much to my grandparents, James Jones Sr., Thelma Jones, and the late Anna Johnson, who since I was born enveloped me in love and prayer. My brother, Marcus Vickers, has been an unwavering source of love, affection, and delightful Beyoncé updates that provided a much-needed respite during my writing process. I also thank my loving cousins: Shaleah, Greg, Hakim, DJ, Damar, Enyjjah, Erin, Kendall, Shayla, Tanisha. I would like to especially thank my cousin Joyce Ray, who was the first person to encourage me to pursue a PhD. And to my fifth grade teacher who is like a member of the family, Frank Shelley, thank you for the years of support.

My husband, Efrain Guerrero, has been an unwavering source of encouragement and support throughout this entire journey. Not only has he been my biggest cheerleader, he has also been one of my most discerning critics. I appreciate you so much. You graciously provided me with the freedom and emotional space to navigate the myriad emotions that accompany the process of writing a book. I am also very thankful for your commitment to taking on the morning shift of walking our beloved dog, Mrs. Carter, to enable me to start my writing days early. Our love story has not only brought me personal and professional growth but has also allowed me to embrace and become part of a vibrant extended family. To the Guerrero clan—Efrain Sr., Imelda, Alejandra, JP, Adriana, Carlos, and Janessa—please accept my heartfelt love. And thank you to my dog, Mrs Carter, who first came into my life during the final stages of my doctoral program. She has been the best companion, cuddler, and comfort during this long, long journey.

I owe everything I am today to my mom, Marian Johnson. She ingrained in me the importance of education and went above and beyond to ensure I had the opportunity to attend the best schools. I can still recall a vivid memory of driving with her as a child, and her pointing toward Central High School, telling me that one day I would be attending there. This school, being the second-oldest public high school in the country and the most prestigious in Philadelphia, would not have been possible without her constant support and guidance. She has invested so much in me and I aspire to be a loving parent like her one day.

I am grateful for everyone in every aspect of my life who helped me. But above all else, I thank God. My faith sustained me throughout this process. I started each day before I wrote reading a spiritual devotional. My faith grounded me, assuaged my anxiety, and taught me I could do anything, including write a whole book, through Christ who strengthens me. So I knew even though I was writing alone, I wasn't. Knowing this made all the difference. It's *how I got over*.

MY ENGAGEMENT WITH Congress began in 2006, when I was selected as a Congressional Black Caucus Foundation summer intern. For nearly eight weeks, I worked for my local representative, Chaka Fattah, who represented Philadelphia for over a decade. I naively thought that I would interact a lot with the Rep that summer, however, most of my time was spent with other staffers in the office, who managed my internship experience. They taught me the ins and outs of the legislative process by allowing me to work closely with them on substantive assignments. They were kind and generous with their time. I developed a deep respect for them as the people who manifested the Rep's agenda. They were the ones who researched and wrote legislation, drafted press statements, answered messages from constituents, and developed strategies to make the Rep's political vision come true. I came to understand that they and other congressional staffers were principal actors in lawmaking.

I continued interning for the Rep from 2006 to 2008 while I was an undergraduate at the George Washington University. This extended work experience gave me more time to observe staff dynamics. For example, I frequently visited different offices to obtain lawmakers' signatures for official letters. I would wait in the reception area of each office while staff provided an official signature. While I waited, I would glance at the photographs and awards that adorned walls, eat the unique candies that each office proudly offered as products from their districts, and listen to conversations within earshot. I would also take note of the social characteristics of who worked in each office and the different levels of racial representation among staff. Representative Fattah, who is Black, had a primarily Black staff. However, I rarely saw Black staffers when I visited White lawmakers' offices. Those offices were mostly White. I began to think about how such different configurations of racial representation among staff affected lawmaking, especially since I had come to understand the influential role of legislative staff.

In 2009, I decided to intern in another congressional office to get a different experience from what I had known. I interned for a White lawmaker, who unsurprisingly had a primarily White staff. My internship experience in this office was completely different, including my relationship with staff. In Representative Fattah's office I was treated as a valued member of the team. Even the staff in his district office knew me. To them I was more than just the perennial intern (our internal joke about my long tenure in the office). They knew about my interests, ambitions, and skills. However, in this new office I was just an intern, and one of many. I was only expected to answer the phone and respond to constituent mail. To be sure, these are all typical intern duties. However, these were tasks that I had rarely completed before, in part because my old office took the time to get to know me, evaluated what I could do, and offered me numerous opportunities for professional growth. They allowed me to research and track legislation and attend policy meetings with other Democratic staffers. I really lucked out with my first office. The day-to-day activities of most Hill interns more closely resemble my second internship experience, regardless of the lawmaker or the racial composition of their staff. Nonetheless, the different cultures in these offices each had an impact on my development as a young Black professional.

The disjuncture between the two internship experiences was demoralizing. In one office I was nurtured and in the other I was ignored. I dreaded coming to work, and when I did,

I volunteered for any assignment that would get me out of the office. I would quickly step forward to take a letter to be signed or pick up a flag that had flown over the Capitol for a constituent. During these errands I would return to my old office for a moment of reprieve to cope with these feelings of boredom and loneliness. While I wandered through the halls, I began practicing common cultural gestures, like the *Black Nod*, to establish a connection with other Black staffers. I found myself nodding to other Black staffers, many of whom were strangers to me, to fortify my strength to just complete the workday and the remaining weeks of my internship. At this time, I wondered how other Black staffers felt in their offices. Did they experience the isolation and unfulfillment that I did in a majority-White office? This time around, I left Congress disenchanted and with more questions than answers about the legislature as an institution.

My congressional internship experiences planted the seeds for *The Last Plantation*. It provided me with an up-close lesson of the powerful role congressional staff hold in lawmaking. It also taught me how race and racism were organizing features in their careers and the everyday occurrences of our national legislature.

THE LAST PLANTATION

Introduction

It has been slave labor on the Hill for years for Blacks who have had no upward mobility, no chance for better working conditions. Congress might be exempt from those laws, but we must make sure that our employees are treated equally and fairly.

    —REPRESENTATIVE HAROLD FORD SR., 1989[1]

This is a rich White man's place.

    —JOSEPH, BLACK CONGRESSIONAL STAFFER

THE UNITED STATES Congress is known as the "Last Plantation." You will not find this inglorious moniker in any of the many introductory texts that survey America's history, nor does it appear in any advanced readings about legislative studies. You will not hear this nickname parlayed among political scientists. But it is a name used widely and often by the people who know Congress most intimately—lawmakers of both parties and their sizable and powerful staffs. In designating Congress as the last plantation, these congressmen, staff, and even reporters were, perhaps unknowingly and unwittingly, identifying what I argue is a central dynamic in preserving America's racial hierarchy.

Drawing on my own experience as a congressional staffer, along with more than seventy-five interviews, I make a three-part argument in this book. First, that racism and race have formed and maintained a racial hierarchy in the heart of our nation's most important lawmaking body. Second, that congressional staffers substantively shape legislation and policy outcomes that are largely underplayed, unappreciated, and overall absent in the literature. Third and relatedly, that the racial hierarchy within the congressional workplace, combined with the outsized power of Congressional staffers, plays a significant role in instantiating White supremacy in federal law and throughout American politics.

While the existence of this congressional "plantation" is in some ways glaringly obvious—members of Congress are overwhelmingly White; their aides equally homogenous; and low-paid service workers are mostly Black and Latino—this hierarchy is in other ways quite invisible to the American public.[2] The structure and ethos of Congress make it convenient for congressional workers to be invisible, obscuring their identity, labor, and existence. These staffers work behind the scenes writing legislation, organizing hearings, and maintaining the Capitol. They are the machinery, mechanisms, and glue that make Congress work! While there is certainly much that they do that is influential, and invisible, I show throughout this book how racism is an even more powerful—and even less visible—force that effectively governs Congress. Racism shapes the work of congressional staffers, impacting who works there, what they do, how they do it, and what kinds of careers and lives they will go on to lead. Most vitally, I argue that by governing the lives and careers of congressional staffers, racism shapes Congress and the entire American political system. The result is that racial inequality is an inherent part of the daily work of Congress, and it meaningfully shapes the work Congress does—the laws they pass; the deals they broker; and the lived realities of the American people.

The roots of the last plantation nickname are deep and knotted but also quite simple: the thousands of people who are employed by Congress—from the senators' aides to the janitors and cooks who make their lives possible—were not covered by the legal workplace protections that cover every other American worker. Congress has written and passed numerous laws that improve the lives and the careers of the American worker, though inequalities in our culture remain abundant, and though there are certain realms of life—like income and wealth distribution—where things are getting worse rather than better.[3] The last century of American law contains a clear direction when it comes to the rights of workers. The first and most noticeable of these was New Deal legislation in the 1930s that established a minimum wage, standardized work hours, and emboldened unions to counter unbridled capitalism. Then in 1964 came the Civil Rights Act, which outlawed discrimination and removed barriers from the workplace for people of color, extending these protections to White women as well as immigrant and religious minorities. As a result of the 1964 Civil Rights Act, American workplaces grew more diverse. White women and people of color, who were previously excluded from professional workplaces or assigned to the most junior roles, gained entry into new professions and ascended into senior roles.[4] While progress from this legislation has been uneven, private and nonprofit workplaces undoubtedly became more egalitarian as a result.[5] After the Civil Rights Act, Congress moved to assure safe and healthy working conditions for men and women by setting and enforcing tough standards.

Across the twentieth century Congress passed numerous laws that applied to other employers but not to itself.[6] Lawmakers argued that they had to preserve the separation of powers between two branches of the federal government to ensure they remained equal. Lawmakers worried that the executive branch, which enforces federal workplace regulations, would not only oversee the congressional workplace, but, more dangerously, would begin to regulate congressional power. Their answer to this imagined constitutional conundrum was for Congress to exempt itself from federal workplace laws. As a consequence, congressional workers were denied, again and again and again, the increasingly expanded set of rights that federal law guaranteed to every other American worker. This is until lawmakers passed the Congressional Accountability Act in 1995, which applied eleven federal workplace laws to the legislative branch.

Beginning in the 1970s, Black congressional employees and a handful of courageous lawmakers drew attention to widespread racial and gender discrimination in the congressional workplace. They pointed to an unequal distribution of staff positions along racial lines, unfair salary practices, and inequity in safety standards among workers in the Capitol. These workers and lawmakers argued that since congressional workers were exempt from the protections of federal workplace laws, Congress was one of the last places where you could still discriminate and exploit workers without legal ramifications. In a new racial epoch committed to equal opportunity and antidiscrimination, Congress was an outlier—it was the only institution to survive our racist past unchanged. Black employees began referring to their place of work as "the last plantation."[7] In 1978, Ohio Senator John Glenn became the first lawmaker to use the term on the record. During a Senate hearing about the handling of discrimination complaints, he said, "No longer can the Congress of the United States be viewed as the 'last plantation' where anything goes."[8] The name stuck. And almost fifty years later, it still applies. The Capitol is an overwhelmingly White space.

Black Capital

In White spaces such as Congress, Black people carve out spaces for themselves. In *The Last Plantation*, I show how Black workers hold and create agency to shape their own destinies and confront White domination. Throughout this book I will explore the many ways Black people in the Capitol use Congress to fight racism rather than entrench it. Though Black lawmakers are a part of these contestations, their contributions and accomplishments are well recorded.[9] There is a much larger story of Black capital that needs to be told. It is the story of Black workers' invisible labor in the Capitol. Black workers are not elected; they cast no legislative votes. However, they are important actors both in showing how Congress is a racialized institution and also how that institution can be altered from within.[10] While I will focus on the careers and experiences of Black staffers specifically, Black workers employed in service and auxiliary roles also labor to keep the capital running. The story of Black people in the Capitol would be incomplete without them. Black service workers challenge racism in the Capitol too. In fact, they did it first, because, for over a century, these were the only positions on the Hill available to Black men and women. What's more, the fates of Black staffers and service workers are intertwined and key to understanding how Congress has transformed as a racialized institution over the last century.

I offer Black capital as a conceptual framework to identify and explain the power and agency of Black congressional workers. Black workers' efforts to recruit other Black men and women to the congressional workplace and adaptive strategies that nurture and affirm group membership and belonging is Black capital. Black capital, as a form of labor and practice of value creation as well as a quality of social and cultural capital, encompasses Black workers' expertise and ingenuity, particularly that which they use to advance legislative work as well as their own collective efforts to make the congressional workplace more inclusive, fair, and just.[11] At the same time, Black capital, like all capital, is context dependent and expresses the relational *and* spatial dimensions of Black political power.[12] It is based upon a Black epistemology that recognizes the extraordinary contributions of everyday Black folks and that captures the multitude of ways they understand and use power.[13] Black capital is a form of social capital amplified by the processes and conditions of Black labor in government. It is seminal to claims for Black freedom and racial justice on the Hill and across the nation. Consequently, this framework offers a more expansive view of American racial formations, particularly who has power and how it is used in American politics.[14]

The presence of Black workers predates the election of the first Black members of Congress by almost sixty years.[15] Lawmakers employed Black workers first as attendants and messengers in the early nineteenth century, and after the Civil War, they began to hire them in greater numbers to celebrate and cement their new status as citizens just as the first African Americans were elected to Congress.[16] Black employment continued in the Capitol throughout the nadir of Black politics, between 1901 and 1928, when no African Americans served in Congress. In the 1930s, lawmakers hired Black professionals to work in their personal and committee offices.[17] Black workers are witnesses, in other words, to two centuries of racism. They have been the loudest and longest critics of inequity on the Hill as it has a direct impact on their livelihoods. Their careers and experiences make it clear that institutional analyses of Congress that do not account for the constitutive role of racism in legislative history are incomplete. Just as important, their careers prove that change is possible.

There is much we can learn by placing Black workers at the center of legislative analysis. By highlighting Black capital, I aim to broaden how we study Congress. Feminist scholar of Congress Cindy Rosenthal said, "Our understanding of institutions is inextricably bound to the dominant individuals who populate them."[18] I want to change that. In the following chapters, I will focus primarily on the career experiences and activism of Black staffers as well as Black service workers. Both groups point to ways that legislative processes work and that are generally unaccounted for in race-neutral congressional analyses.[19] Existing profiles on congressional staff assume that they are exclusively young or middle-aged White men, and they do not fully account for how race and gender shape professional identities or career trajectories.[20] I aim, through focusing on Black capital, to broaden the conceptual and methodological approaches used in studying Congress by taking a Black epistemological standpoint that recognizes the significance of Black workers as valuable sources of knowledge.

By Black epistemologies, I refer both to the broad corpus of literary and analytical work by Black and Black Studies scholars as well as the lived, everyday ways of knowing and making do that Black people across the country use to get by and to thrive.[21] Black epistemological approaches can reveal theories of knowledge that emanate from the lived experiences of Black men and women. On Capitol Hill, by attending to Black staffers' knowledge and practices through a Black epistemologies approach, I demonstrate how congressional employment is a White racial project and how Black workers' knowledge and actions reorient this project to facilitate racial justice and more inclusive policymaking.

In *The Last Plantation*, I use the plantation metaphor to investigate how Congress operates as an inequality regime.[22] The term coined by sociologist Joan Acker describes how race, gender, and class all act as intersecting and overlapping forces that shape how organizations operate. As she describes, these forces dictate who has power and who does not; workplace decisions that explain how work should be completed; hiring and promotions; salary, rewards, and punishment; respect and authority; and feelings of belongings and nonbelonging.[23] To this end, Joseph, who I quoted in the epigraph, told me Congress was a "plantation." He explained that Whites have the visible face of Congress, but "all the work done behind the scenes is done by Blacks," including most of the cooks and custodians in congressional restaurants.

The congressional workplace is unlike most inequality regimes that sociologists typically study. Congress is Congress! It is an immensely powerful institution, where inequality that is anchored locally has national and global implications. While it is important for us to understand the intersectional nature of legislative inequality, I will focus our attention on its racial underpinning, owing to the extant literature on gender and class in Congress.[24] I build on the work of sociologists of racism like Wendy Leo Moore, Victor Ray, Adia Wingfield, and Celeste Watkins-Hayes, all of whom draw attention to how race is at the center of organizational life.[25] They demonstrate how racism shapes how organizations develop and change; determines positions and salary and consequently rewards and punishments; and influences individuals' behaviors and interactions. Of course, racism does not explain everything that happens in an organization. However, as these scholars point out, it does explain a lot, and for much of our country's history we have been unwilling to acknowledge how much racism does matter. The study of racialized organizations commands our attention to focus on structure and the permanence of racism. I agree with much of this scholarship, but I also want to show how racialized organizations are malleable.[26]

I see Congress in Black and White.[27] It is a space built by enslaved Black laborers and where there have been ten times as many White enslavers to serve in the legislature than Black men and women.[28] A workplace where the namesakes of the office buildings honor White men who have served in Congress and where one building in particular, the Russell Senate Office Building, commemorates an avowed White supremacist.[29] And where insular hiring and promotion processes yield a super majority of Whites in congressional staff positions. At the same time, I see Congress as a space where Black men and women have fought for their right to be included. And once inside, where they continued to fight, standing up to racists and demanding justice. From them, we can see the shortcomings of Congress but also its potential to execute democratic principles.

I develop my argument in two parts by analyzing the career experiences of Black congressional staffers. First, I show how the congressional workplace produces inequality. Lawmakers' decisions to exempt themselves from the regulations they impose on other employers have led to insular hiring and management decisions that perpetuate racial inequality. They have created and managed an unequal workplace where positions are racially stratified, space is segregated, and identities and interactions are racialized. This hierarchy constrains the agency of non-White staffers and reinforces the credentialing of a White power elite. Second, I demonstrate how Black workers—from legislative staffers to cafeteria servers—have fought back against these unequal work processes and injustices on Capitol

Hill. I show how Black workers have reimagined Congress as a *Black capitol*, a site of minority empowerment where they use their institutional positions, however marginal they might be, to promote racial justice.

Legislative Work and the Reproduction of Racism

Previous research has examined the duties and responsibilities of legislative staff and investigated whether this group is made up of mere passive agents who support their political bosses, or if this unelected class exercises independent effects on the policymaking process.[30] However, rather than looking at the power that legislative staff hold individually, it is important to consider how power is distributed within this large work system and how it affects democratic governance and political representation more broadly. Put simply, it matters (substantively and symbolically) how work opportunities are allocated in a national lawmaking institution.

Most Americans, myself included, are unaware of the sophisticated ecosytem that exists under the iconic neoclassical dome and how it functions day to day. I was so overwhelmed when I first stepped inside the Capitol as a summer intern in 2006. The Capitol was much, much bigger than I expected. I had thought a lot about what it would be like to step onto the House floor for the first time or visit a hearing room in the Senate, but I did not really consider how Capitol Hill was a world unto itself, similar in size to my university campus only three miles away. There are the personal offices of 535 elected officials and six nonvoting members; dozens of committees; support and administrative offices; flex spaces that host staff meetings, professional development seminars, and receptions; a sprawling visitors center; several restaurants, delis, and convenience stores; office supply stores; dry cleaners; cell phone providers; a childcare center; barbershops and hair salons; post offices; congressional credit unions; and two members-only gyms. There is even an underground subway system that connects the office buildings to the Capitol and an independent power plant that provides chilled and steamed water to cool and heat offices. Walking from one end of the Capitol to the other, which requires traversing different elevations, is tiresome, and I quickly learned if you are working or visiting the Hill, you better wear comfortable shoes.

The cognitive dissonance I experienced was jarring, but looking back, it was quite understandable. We look at Congress from a front-stage perspective, as it has been grandly depicted on postcards, the fifty dollar bill, and the news. We observe lawmakers in highly dramatized moments like voting, hearings, and speeches against the backdrop of stately ceremonial rooms. However, we do not see all the preparation that goes on backstage across a vast setting and from an array of workers who produce the moments we watch on cable news or social media. This prominent but simplified view not only obscures the size of Congress but hides all the people who work on the Hill.

After my first week on the Hill, I was not sure if I would ever learn how to navigate this place. The Capitol complex includes six office buildings, three each for the House and Senate. To the south sit the Rayburn, Longworth, and Cannon House office buildings. The Senate side is north of the Capitol building. It includes the Russell, Dirksen, and Hart office buildings. Lawmakers have their personal offices in multiroom suites, which vary in size. The personal offices of freshmen representatives can be cramped. Reception areas sometimes double as conference rooms, and aides work side by side in cramped rooms of policy and communications staff. By contrast, senior representatives have more spacious and private office accommodations that can be twice as large. Senators have the largest offices of all, some of which span multiple floors. From the outside, all the neoclassical buildings look distinguished and orderly. However, inside is a different story—it is chaotic. In the summer months, the hallways swell with new intern cohorts and tourists who collide with the usual mix of lawmakers, workers, and K Street lobbyists. It is hard to orient yourself in this sea of dark-hued suits, and it is made more difficult by the unique layout of each building. Navigating the long hallways feels like a maze, and the cacophony of clacking heels, fast-paced conversations, and the deafening buzzers that alert lawmakers to their voting schedule only add to this confusion. Learning the physical layout of the Capitol takes time. However, what truly defines Congress is not its buildings or the rooms inside, but the people who work there.

The congressional workforce is divided between two groups: staffers who work directly for lawmakers in their personal, committee, and leadership offices, and an army of auxiliary workers who handle the administrative and physical operations of the Capitol. This last group includes police officers, groundskeepers, custodians, food workers, and non-partisan professionals. Many of these workers are employed by the Architect of the Capitol, the federal agency responsible for the maintenance, operation, and preservation of the Capitol Complex. In addition, the clerk of the House and secretary of the Senate employ a range of nonpartisan professionals like stenographers, curators, HR professionals, and historians to handle legislative, financial, and administrative functions. Ultimately, Congress might look like a singular institution from the outside looking in, but in reality, it is a highly fragmented work organization with over thirty thousand workers employed across hundreds of offices.

Senators and representatives oversee all the different agencies and offices that handle day-to-day operations and personnel management as well as their own personal staffs. As such, lawmakers are responsible for the management and well-being of all Capitol workers. Ultimately, they have final say about what happens on Capitol Hill. Managing a work organization this size is no easy job, especially when the task of overseeing legislative branch workers often comes a distant second to legislating itself. The rules that govern this entire system have evolved haphazardly, and as I will show in the next chapter, produce inequality among workers.

In this book, I focus on the careers and experiences of congressional staffers. Lawmakers employ on average fourteen staffers in the House and forty-nine staffers in the Senate in their personal offices to assist them with representation, oversight, and policymaking work. Congressional staff are split between DC and state offices. Staffers in state offices primarily handle constituent services, whereas DC staff juggle policy and political work. Although congressional office structure varies, a typical office is organized by senior, mid-level, and junior roles.

At the top of any congressional office chain of command—aside from the lawmaker—is the chief of staff. They hire, promote, and terminate staff; establish office protocols; and provide political and policy guidance. Other senior staffers include legislative directors and communications directors who manage policy and press operations, respectively. Legislative directors oversee lawmakers' policy portfolios and closely monitor what happens on the floor. They provide vote recommendations and consequently must have a working knowledge of a vast swath of policy issues and institutional procedures. They work closely with communications directors who shape their boss's voice externally through strategic messaging and with the goal of helping them stand out in a crowded chamber. To this end, communication directors help lawmakers create, refine, and amplify their positions on a national stage. Top staffers have a lot of power and influence. They are often the last individuals lawmakers speak to right before they cast any vote. What's more, it is these individuals who fill in for lawmakers when they are busy, and for these reasons, political scientist Michael Malbin describes them as *unelected representatives* because they have the power to make executive decisions when their bosses are unavailable.[31] In American politics, access is everything and something elites try to buy.[32] Which is why top staffers, who have deep relationships with our nation's elected leaders, are often recruited by corporations to further their agendas.

Next, mid-level staff hold positions like legislative assistants, legislative counsels, and policy advisors. These staffers are heavily involved in legislative work. They are lawmakers' eyes and ears. They meet with different stakeholders, research and write legislation, and monitor legislative action, all of which allow them to provide recommendations for how a lawmaker should act.

Finally, junior staffers include staff assistants, legislative correspondents, and schedulers. They handle the administrative business of congressional offices and have limited policy roles. In addition, fellows and interns assist with this work. Interns and fellows can have either paid or unpaid roles. If you have ever called, written, or visited your member of Congress, it was probably one of these junior staffers with whom you interacted. It is tempting to view junior staffers as people without power, but everyone on the Hill has power. What's more, as I will discuss in chapter 2, the pathway from a junior staffer to a more senior role is very short. In the span of a couple years, a staff assistant can become a legislative director.

This is why obtaining one of these entry-level roles can be highly competitive.

In addition to personal office staffers, there are committee staffers. Committees, led by staff directors, are where most legislation originates these days.[33] Committee staffers generally have advanced degrees and expertise in the committee's jurisdiction. These roles are highly sought after because of the substantive opportunities to shape policy. Lastly, there are the staffers who work directly for congressional leaders like the Speaker of the House and the Senate majority leader. Leadership staffers provide strategy and guidance for party leaders and help them manage their caucus. They also help organize the House and Senate Floor schedules, message party goals, and liaise with the executive branch.

This book grapples with fundamental questions about the role that Congress plays in shaping the US racial order, the overarching system that puts Whites on top and everyone else, including Black and Brown people, on the bottom. The dominant explanation of the Capitol's role in American racial formations is that lawmakers structure the racial order, for better or worse, through public policy.[34] For example, social scientists have focused on how lawmakers constructed a social welfare system that primarily benefited Whites and a mass incarceration apparatus that disproportionately punished non-Whites.[35] The impact of public policy cannot be overstated. But what is far less acknowledged is the vast, although far more subtle, impact of the people our lawmakers chose to hire.

The people who lawmakers hire are then the people who help them construct the laws they write and negotiate the bills that they try to pass. They are the people who lawmakers trust and empower. They are also overwhelmingly White. Recent policy reports show that people of color are significantly underrepresented in top staff positions like chiefs of staff, communication directors, and legislative directors. For example, although people of color make up over 40 percent of the national population, they only account for 18 percent of top staff, like chiefs of staff, communications directors, and legislative directors in the House and 11 percent of top staff in the Senate.[36] The underrepresentation of communities of color is shameful. It is also highly problematic for an institution whose core responsibility is to represent Americans' diverse interests.

Congressional employment, as it exists, represents an unofficial policy statement about who gets to participate in government. As it is written now, it is primarily for Whites only. The underrepresentation of people of color is a unique form of marginalization through which they are excluded from making racial policy that is then imposed on the nation. Congress thus shapes the US racial order in two ways: through the creation of public policy and the cultivation of political professionals. In both respects, lawmakers have tremendous power to structure social inequality. While they can use their lawmaking powers to diminish preexisting inequalities, they have too often used their legislative perch to exacerbate and create new forms of inequality. Analyzing Congress as a workplace and legislative work as a labor practice reveals the hidden and more enduring forms of what I term *legislative inequality*. I define legislative inequality as the intricate interplay of both explicit and implicit mechanisms that govern the distribution of roles, positions, and responsibilities within Congress, wherein race, gender, and social class collectively and individually shape the composition and dynamics of the workforce, as well as the manner in which legislative tasks are undertaken. This encompasses insular hiring practices and nontransparent management decisions that mold the contours of the congressional workplace as well as pervasive patterns of spatial segregation and day-to-day interactions inside the

Capitol, which convey symbolic messages of inclusion and exclusion.

On Capitol Hill, the unequal distribution of resources and rewards among workers produces legislative inequality.[37] This process happens across multiple stages. Lawmakers have wide discretion in who they can hire, and as we will learn in the next chapter, they have not always abided by the same rules that private employers must follow to promote equal opportunity and antidiscrimination. Most of the people they hire are White and a few are people of color. But then those people of color have a harder time getting in and rising in the ranks. Thus, inequality surfaces twice, first in hiring decisions and again in how the people who are hired are rewarded and promoted. As a result, the congressional workplace is a White-dominated organization marked by barriers and insular hiring practices that promote and legitimate racial stratification among political professionals.

Racial equity in these jobs is essential because they are the embodiment of political power. First, lawmakers could not fulfill their vast responsibilities without congressional staffers. Lawmakers have very busy schedules. When they are in DC, their days are jam-packed with meetings from sunrise to sunset. On any given day they are meeting with their staff, interest groups, lobbyists, and government officials; speaking to groups visiting from their home state and at special events; attending committee hearings; and voting on legislation. The topics of all these meetings, hearings, and votes are different, which requires one to two staffers following behind the member briefing them about what is coming next. Additionally, a substantial amount of their time is spent fundraising for their next election. Fundraising is a job itself.[38] These busy days barely leave lawmakers with enough time to eat, let alone think, and consequently leaves staffers to do the substantive legislative work that lawmakers cannot. This gives congressional staff a tremendous amount of responsibility. Staff must develop and enact their boss's agenda, which includes researching policy issues; reviewing and developing legislative proposals; and collaborating and coordinating with other congressional offices. These are all important components of the legislative process that staffers complete and piece together. However, unequal racial representation among staffers means that it is mostly Whites who conduct the nation's legislative business.

Second, congressional staff's vast responsibilities give them a lot of influence. Senior and mid-level staffers, in particular, have a lot of sway. As staffers gain seniority and acquire more expertise and institutional knowledge, their roles shift from just doing what their bosses tell them to helping lawmakers think about what they should do overall. In a deeply polarized and highly competitive environment, lawmakers rely on their most senior aides to help them decide what to do and how to stand out. Staffers, especially those on committees, guide lawmakers based upon their deep knowledge of complicated policy issues and their understanding of existing federal law. Additionally, top staffers provide advice from surveying the latest developments, locally and nationally, and identify opportunities to advance a lawmaker's reputation and agenda. As I will show in chapter 4, senior and mid-level staffers guide lawmakers in developing their uncrystallized agendas. Of course, the extent to which members of Congress rely on their staff exists on a continuum. Some lawmakers have brilliant political minds and provide their staff with clear directions to enact a well-thought-out and defined agenda. By contrast, some members rely on their staff a great deal. Freshmen members rely on veteran staffers to teach them the ropes when they first enter Congress.[39] Additionally, some long-serving members require more hands-on support from their staff as well as lawmakers who become temporarily incapacitated due to health issues while serving.[40] But overall, the overrepresentation of Whites in senior and mid-level staff positions means that is mainly Whites who are setting and negotiating political agendas, which is problematic for our multiracial democracy.

Third, congressional employment provides staffers entry into an elite institution and unrestricted access to the nation's leaders. These jobs, even the most junior positions, provide workers with the opportunity to meet, interact, and develop relationships with decision-makers. What's more, staffers acquire social capital from their relationships with each other. Time and time again, I observed that if you want to get something done on the Hill it depends on who you know.

Congressional employment trains, socializes, and credentials political talent. On Capitol Hill, congressional staffers acquire issue expertise, develop social relationships with other political elites, and learn the intimate dimensions of policy-making and politicking. Imbued with these resources, congressional staff leave Capitol Hill for more influential political positions. In this way, the congressional workplace is a training ground and subsequent feeder institution to other elite political workplaces. These future career paths include journeys to elected office as well as senior roles in the executive and judicial branches, political campaigns, lobbying and consulting, and the nonprofit and advocacy sectors.[41] Inequality that begins within the walls of the Capitol expands outward throughout Washington, DC, and across the nation through the dissemination of a White power elite.[42]

The unequal racial makeup of congressional staff is one of the most important problems subverting our multiracial democracy. The effects are multiple. It enshrines a racial hierarchy within Congress itself when it is supposed to be the federal branch of government most representative of the nation. It undermines the entire legislative process from start to finish, amplifying the experiences and preferences of Whites in policy discussions, and ultimately in federal law, while marginalizing communities of color. Finally, it empowers and credentials an unrepresentative group to participate in American politics at an even more influential level in their future jobs. Congressional employment has been a mechanism to instantiate White supremacy at deep levels for decades.

Methods

For this book, I interviewed seventy-eight current and former congressional staffers between 2010 and 2015. The majority of these individuals were Black (53 percent). Women made up 47 percent of this sample. Collectively, these staffers had a rich set of experiences. They worked directly for lawmakers in their personal offices (in Washington and back home); in committees; and in leadership and other supporting offices. Through their careers they occupied multiple roles within and across offices. Accordingly, among this group, 49 percent were top senior staffers like chiefs of staff, legislative directors, and communications directors; 39 percent were mid-level staff like legislative assistants; and 12 percent held junior roles like staff assistants and interns. In addition, 47 percent had experiences working for a Black lawmaker and 49 percent had worked for a White lawmaker.

I conducted the majority of interviews on Capitol Hill. I would meet staff wherever and whenever they were able to meet, mindful of their busy and unpredictable schedules. Sometimes this meant coming to them and meeting in their boss's private office during a recess period. These were special moments where they could reflect quietly, surrounded by ceremonial furnishings and political memorabilia, about their presence in a powerful institution. Many times, their offices were crowded, so we would go downstairs to a cafeteria in the basement. We would always try to find a quiet space, but that was not always possible. Those moments brought to mind how Congress is a busy workplace, and staffers sought to explain how they fit into this complex system. Lastly, to speak with former staffers, I ventured to their new offices, often along the K Street business corridor in Washington. These corporate offices did not have the grandeur of a state building, but as lobbyists and consultants these former staffers now had their own private space and the luxury of not worrying about time as they reflected on their old jobs. Wherever I met a staffer I was eager to learn about their career and political perspectives.

I started these conversations asking them how they got their start—probing about what drew them to the Hill, how they found their initial position, whether they did this alone or with assistance, their initial impressions of the legislature, and the journey from one role to the next. Next, I had them explain their jobs. Here, I was interested in learning about the influence of congressional staff in lawmaking. That is, how their own ideas and racial and gender identity affected their work, and, ultimately, their boss's legislative agenda. For junior staffers, their responsibilities were straightforward; they did mostly administrative work. However, mid-level and senior staffers had an active role guiding policymaking. Additionally, with chiefs of staff I inquired about how they recruited and hired staff, especially as it related to the racial and gender composition of their office. Finally, I asked what it was like to work day to day in Congress. I inquired about their relationships and social interactions with peers and lawmakers. It was during the latter half of these approximately hour-long conversations that we would discuss the role of race, and also gender and class. As I will show, race shaped how they saw their position within

Congress and how they approached their roles and relationships with other Hill workers and lawmakers. Overall, this approach allows me to offer a sociological explanation to how Congress works, which, in many ways, builds on the earlier work of political scientists studying the legislature.[43]

Staffers of color were very candid about their racial experiences and highlighted the structural elements of racism on the Hill.[44] This, in turn, shaped how I wrote this book. Congressional staffers are not supposed to make news or speak out about what is wrong in their offices. When staffers spoke to me, they were breaking norms and taking a risk to make the institution better. Exposing these truths could have serious repercussions on their careers, even though I spoke to them years ago. In far too many instances, there are Black men and women who are instantly identifiable by just listing their title. That is how White Washington politics is. For this reason, I do not use staffers' real names in this book. What's more, what I have learned consistently throughout this project is that racism is a persistent problem on Capitol Hill. Calling out an individual lawmaker or political party obscures how racism is built into the foundations of Congress, figuratively and literally. When I interviewed Black staffers who worked on the Hill, some as early as the 1970s, I was struck by how little had changed—from hiring processes to the racial composition of the congressional workforce. To show how this problem manifests from one session of Congress to next, I only occasionally reference individual lawmakers. When mentioning an individual by both their first and last name, I am using their actual name. On the other hand, when I use only a first name, it is a pseudonym I've assigned to someone to maintain their privacy.

Throughout this book, I also draw upon ethnographic observations and archival research. During the summers of 2010–13, I worked as a legislative intern in my old congressional office.

This position allowed me to observe congressional culture up close and embed myself in staff networks. I attended meetings of various Black staff associations, which are equivalent to affinity groups in the corporate sector. These meetings illustrated the realities and concerns of Black staffers, and, more importantly, demonstrated this group as a community.

As I mentioned in the prologue, the genesis of this project is shaped by my own racial experiences as a young Black man when I interned on the Hill in college. My racial identity and Hill experience helped me penetrate staff networks, which are traditionally closed to outsiders. One of my last interviews was with a Black Republican who worked as a staffer in the 1980s. He confided to me that he only agreed to speak with me because of a referral from another staffer and because I was a "brotha" doing a PhD at Columbia (which he knew was difficult and so he wanted to be a resource). Without those two things, he would have blown me off. Herbert Gans, the esteemed sociologist and ethnographer, encouraged me to be in people's faces while doing fieldwork because it would be harder for them to tell me "no" when I was standing in front of them. He was right. I still received many rejections doing this project. But it was through the support and generosity of Black staff that I was able to complete this project.

Overview

In the forthcoming chapters, I use the careers of Black workers to show how the congressional workplace is an inequality regime. In chapter 1, I detail the origins of this unequal system. I argue that the main reason why inequality persists in the congressional workplace, even from one session of Congress to the next, is that lawmakers are exempt from federal workplace law and accountable to almost no one in how they manage a vast army of workers. As lawmakers have tried to comply with federal law, I highlight how in practice they still do not follow the same rules they have mandated all other work employers follow. In chapter 2, I focus on how the inequality regime operates in the individual offices through staff recruitment and hiring. Here I give attention to the insular hiring practices that yield a White-dominated workplace and that shut many Black professionals out.

After describing the racialized structure of Congress and how difficult it is for job seekers to penetrate, I explore in chapter 3 what it feels like day-to-day to be inside. I analyze a common cultural practice within the Black community, nodding, as a way of seeing the racial landscape on the Hill. Indeed, for Black Americans in Congress, the nod is a way of seeing one another. Next, I focus on how Black staffers challenge legislative inequality. In chapter 4, I show how they counter Whiteness in legislative work by engaging in inclusive policymaking (that is how they represent diverse and marginalized interests). In chapter 5, I highlight Black staffers' work to diversify the congressional workplace and draw public attention to this problem. Finally, I conclude with policy recommendations to address legislative inequality.

CHAPTER ONE

Do as I Say Not as I Do

HOW CONGRESS REMAINS ABOVE THE LAW

People on Capitol Hill don't even enjoy basic human rights. There's no overtime pay; some people don't even get vacations. A lot of people who get sick just get fired. There's not even any provision for maternity leave. I think they [members of Congress] like having serfs working for them.

—UNNAMED WOMAN STAFFER, 1978[1]

A HUNDRED YEARS ago there were no Black members of Congress. Legal disenfranchisement coupled with White racist violence sharply curtailed Black political participation and vanquished Black lawmakers from the Capitol. George H. White, the last Black representative elected during Reconstruction, said in his farewell address in 1901 that this is "perhaps the Negroes' temporary farewell to the American Congress; but . . . phoenix-like he will rise up some day and come again." His premonition proved true. In the 118th Congress (2023–24), there are sixty-three Black lawmakers, the largest the group has ever been. In the House, 14 percent of representatives are Black, equal to the share of Black Americans. In addition, there are also more Latino, Asian, and Indigenous lawmakers than ever before. Since 2010, members of Congress have consistently grown more racially and ethnically diverse than the previous session. In the 118th Congress, 25 percent of House and Senate members were people of color. This is a remarkable achievement in our endeavor toward a more representative, multiracial democracy.

Today we celebrate the election of a record-setting number of lawmakers of color as a demonstration that we have overcome a dark chapter in our nation's past. At the start of every new Congress, there are awe-inspiring profiles of newly elected lawmakers who ran successful campaigns articulating bold policy ideas and a change agenda. Pictures of these racially diverse cohorts are widely circulated in the news, television, and on social media platforms. These news articles and the commentary that ensues suggest that Congress is transforming from a White space to one more inclusive and representative of the nation.

However, as much as Congress has changed, a lot has remained the same. When you peer beneath the surface you see an institution that remains far from representative of the nation and that is still guided by unequal processes. For instance, although Congress is more racially diverse than it has ever been, it is still an institution dominated by Whites. White men and women constitute 60 percent of the national population but account for 75 percent of lawmakers. What's more, unequal racial representation is even more pronounced in the congressional workplace.

People of color are dramatically underrepresented in senior staff roles like chiefs of staff, communications directors, and legislative directors. Senior staffers are lawmakers' most trusted advisors and their perspective matters. Whether it is on COVID-19 and the economy or criminal justice reform and algorithmic biases, lawmakers turn to their senior aides to educate them about how these pressing issues affect their districts and states and to make appropriate recommendations. Senior staffers also frequently bring relevant issues to lawmakers' attention that they are unaware of. If there are few staffers of color in the room, it will be harder for lawmakers, who are disproportionately White, to understand how communities of color, which account for over 40 percent of the national population, are uniquely impacted by these social problems.

In 2015, I published a policy paper for the Joint Center for Political and Economic Studies that showed people of color only occupied 7 percent of top staff roles in the Senate.[2] The report was newsworthy because it was the first report in over a decade to empirically document how people of color were underrepresented in these leading roles. As I will discuss later in this chapter, tracking who holds these positions is not easy. I used personnel records to find photographs of top staffers online and make racial classifications, a method that was less than ideal but necessary given the nontransparency of Congress. The report received widespread news attention, including coverage by the *Washington Post* and *The Atlantic*.[3] A follow-up report conducted by LaShonda Brenson showed that in 2020 people of color only held 11 percent of top staff positions in the Senate.[4] She found that Senate offices that represent states with large Black and Latino populations continued to hire relatively few Black and Latino senior staffers. While there has been some progress in staffers of color gaining influence in Senate office, the rate of change has been incremental and still leaves communities of color underrepresented.

Racial representation among senior staff in the House isn't much better even though House lawmakers are much more racially diverse. In 2022, the Joint Center found that people of color hold 18 percent of all top staff positions in the House.[5] In the offices of White Democratic members, 14.8 percent of top staffers are people of color. Comparatively, in the offices of White Republican members, 5.1 percent of top staffers are people of color. Racialized gerrymandering contributes to racial segregation in the congressional workforce. White Democrats represent districts that are on average 38.9 percent people of color. Republicans represent districts that are on average 25.9 percent people of color. But racialized gerrymandering does not explain everything. Nearly half of the 239 House members (48.1 percent) who represent districts that are at least one-third people of color do not have a single top staffer of color in their office.

Overall, studies demonstrate that White representatives, Republicans and Democrats alike, hire White staffers for the most influential positions in their offices.[6] In contrast, Black, Latino, and Asian representatives were more likely to hire people of color for these same roles. It is not surprising that there are not many staffers of color leading Republican offices, given the party's open embrace of White supremacy over the last decade and the Whiteness of the Republican caucus. However, we should expect Democratic House offices to look different. The Democratic Party openly celebrates racial diversity and markets itself as the "big tent" party, where voters of all backgrounds are welcomed and respected. More critically, Democratic voters are disproportionately made up of people of color. For example, about one-fifth of Democratic voters are Black Americans. Yet the racially diverse coalitions that get Democratic representatives elected are not reflected in the senior staffers in congressional offices. In all, these data paint a disappointing view of representation in Congress and one that contrasts sharply with our own perceptions of an institution that is changing.

While congressional staff diversity has received notable media attention in recent years, it might surprise you to know that news articles focusing on the overwhelming Whiteness of the congressional workplace go back at least five decades. For example, in 1974, a *Washington Post* columnist wrote, "The total of 28 Blacks in professional jobs in the Senate may sound pathetically small, in view of the fact that there are about 900 professional level jobs in the Senate."[7] As you can see, not much has changed. Despite this media attention, why does racial inequality in the congressional workplace persist from one Congress to the next?

The reasons why people of color are continually underrepresented in congressional staff roles are complex, but the short answer is that the congressional workplace is an *inequality regime*. Sociologist Joan Acker defines an inequality regime as the "interrelated practices, processes, actions, and meanings that result in and maintain class, gender, and racial inequalities within particular organizations."[8] I use this term to describe how race, gender, and class shape who gets jobs on Capitol Hill. This means that diversifying the elected membership of the legislature will not easily solve this problem because so much of this inequality is baked into how Congress works. In addition, high-profile news stories on this subject will not change Congress if it does not focus on the structural roots of inequality. In this chapter, I explain how this inequality regime emerged and remained intact for decades.

A Brief History of Racism in the Capitol

Congress, for most of its history, was an openly racist institution. Lawmakers did not try to hide their racist beliefs and gleefully worked to codify their prejudices into federal law.[9] This racism extends to the organization and management of the congressional workplace.

As we know, during the colonial era, enslaved Black laborers toiled alongside free Blacks and Whites to build the Capitol. They labored in sweltering heat, tormented by mosquitoes, and kept to a grueling pace despite not being directly compensated for their work on weekdays. Philip Reid is the most well-known enslaved laborer who helped construct the Capitol. He ingeniously figured out how to assemble the Statue of Freedom that sits atop the Capitol dome from five disjointed sections that had left others baffled. Reid labored for over a year, seven days a week, and only earned $42 for his work on Sundays to assemble the bronze monument. He gained manumission in 1862, a year before the statue was put on top of the Capitol.[10]

During Reconstruction (1865–77), lawmakers began to directly hire Black men and women, in large numbers, for positions throughout the Capitol. This shift was an acknowledgment of Black Americans' new status as citizens granted by the Fourteenth Amendment. This progress was quickly undone when racist southern lawmakers gained majorities in Congress following Reconstruction.[11] They established a formidable racial caste system within the congressional workplace that began with firing Black men and women from highly visible positions.[12] For example, Southern Democrats attempted to fire William H. Smith, the House librarian and one of the highest-ranking African American employees in Congress. His termination was difficult to enact because he was widely regarded as an expert by Republicans and Democrats. Smith stayed in his position for only two years and was replaced by a Confederate.[13] However, Southern Democrats were more successful firing other high-profile Black men and women, like Robert Downing, the head of the House members' dining room and Kate Brown, a ladies' room attendant in the Senate.[14]

In the decades following Reconstruction, Black workers were exclusively employed in caretaker roles like cooks,

drivers, messengers, and attendants. This arrangement rein-
forced a southern racial order in the Capitol. As a reminder, from
1901 to 1929 there were no Black members of Congress, and
the racially stratified workforce that placed Black workers at
the bottom of the legislative hierarchy is illustrative of how
Congress was organized as a White space.[15]

This racial hierarchy did not begin to change until the
election of Black lawmakers in the 1930s. When Black lawmakers returned, they employed Black men and women in
professional positions to work in their offices. However, Black
legislative staff did not have the same rights as their White
peers. For example, in 1934, Morris Lewis, the executive assistant to Oscar De Priest, the first Black representative elected
since Reconstruction, was denied service in the public House
restaurant. Morris, who was with his young son at the time,
was informed that the restaurant did not serve "Negroes" and
was asked to leave. De Priest forced an investigation into the
restaurant's discriminatory practices. Astonishingly, a House
panel ruled that the public House restaurant was a private
facility set up for the convenience of lawmakers and that discrimination was allowable.[16] Racial segregation in the Capitol
continued for the next two decades. What we see during this
period prior to the Civil Rights Movement is that even as the
number of Black men and women in the Capitol grew, albeit
marginally, racism remained an important organizing factor
that determined access to work opportunities and privileges.

This racist history of the congressional workplace is not
that surprising, as White supremacy was the ruling ideology
for the nation from its inception. White supremacy organized
American workplaces, excluding Black men and women from
the best jobs and assigning them to the worst.[17] Why would
we expect Congress to be different? It is reasonable, however,
to expect that Congress would change as a result of the Civil

Rights Movement—when Black social movements forced lawmakers to pass legislation barring racial discrimination in employment and make job opportunities more equitable. But as we know, racism and inequality persist in the congressional workplace to this day. Why?

Sociological research on racialized institutions is instructive for understanding why racial inequality is so persistent in Congress. For starters, this work demonstrates that racial institutions do not change, they adapt. Sociologists Michael Omi and Howard Winant argue that racialized institutions use two strategies to resolve racialized conflict, absorption, and insulation.[18] Absorption describes how the state responds to racial conflict by accepting and moderating extreme demands from social movements, which allows state leaders to say they are embracing change. In addition, another absorption tactic is the incorporation of people of color into historically White-dominated institutions. This strategy allows these same leaders to exert control over people of color who join the institution and to fracture the coalitions that demand change.[19] For example, consider candidates of color who boldly run for Congress. However, when they are elected and join either the House or Senate, their rhetoric becomes less assertive because they must work with other lawmakers to enact their agenda and answer to party leaders who control their committee assignments and can marginalize them within their caucus. Insulation, on the other hand, represents the symbolic changes made within organizations that signal compliance to civil rights law but that otherwise allow businesses to continue as a normal. For example, Lauren Edelman finds that organizations create visible signs of compliance to antidiscrimination law.[20] However, these laws are defined by broad and ambiguous principles, and it is easy for organizations to avoid changing. It is like an employer who posts equal opportunity flyers throughout the workplace but continues hiring through a small racially exclusive network of friends and family. The employer says they are committed to attracting a diverse workforce, but federal civil rights laws contain no mechanisms to hold employers accountable for not doing so. In the next chapter, I will show how these insular hiring processes similarly unfold on the Hill.

Absorption and insulation are two strategies that keep many organizations White. While Congress is like many other racial institutions where people of color are conspicuously absent from leadership positions, it has additional powers it can use to preserve the status quo. Congress is the site of federal legislative power, where lawmakers make the rules that govern our everyday lives. Accordingly, what sets Congress apart from other inequality regimes is that Congress is a lawmaking institution that is simultaneously exempt from the rules it sets. As I will show, legislative exemption has important consequences for how racism and inequality is maintained on Capitol Hill.

This story begins with the "last plantation" metaphor. As news headlines declared Congress was changing, the metaphor indicated the opposite, that racial inequality was not only present in the halls of the Capitol but that it was entrenched. Proponents of the metaphor identified the source of the problem as exemption from federal workplace laws, rules that promoted antidiscrimination and equal opportunity. But what exemption from these rules really demonstrates is how Congress is a lawmaking institution that is simultaneously above the law. That is, lawmakers have a lot of discretion as employers in their offices, and of the congressional workplace more broadly, to run things as they see fit. Giving up this amount of power is hard and explains why it has been so difficult for lawmakers to comply with federal workplace law. As we will see, even when lawmakers "comply" they do so in ways that preserve their powers over workers' interests. Exemption from the rules at large makes the congressional workplace insular and nontransparent. Together, all of this is what allows racial inequality to persist from one Congress to the next.

A History of Exemption

Ten years after the passage of the Civil Rights Act, which barred racial and gender discrimination in employment, the *Fort Worth Star-Telegram* reported that twenty Hill offices overtly discriminated in staff recruitment.[21] Job advertisements circulated by the Congressional Office of Placement and Office Management expressed lawmakers' hiring preferences that violated the rights of almost all legally protected classes. Representatives William J. Randall (D-MO) and Robert L. Leggett (D-CA) wrote that "no minority" should apply in ads for administrative aides. Representative Vernon Thomson (R-WI) wanted a "White Republican" for a clerk-typist position. What's more, staff in the congressional employment office were instructed to indicate the race of Black job seekers and marked their resumes with a "B."[22]

These job announcements were not just racist, they were sexist as well. Lawmakers sought out women for racialized and gendered roles. Representative Edward P. Boland (D-MA) requested a woman stenographer, adding, "No southern accents, Whites Only." Democratic Florida Representative James A. Haley wanted "only a White girl," preferably from his home state. Pennsylvania Representative Albert Johnson aimed to hire a Republican staffer but added "Doesn't have to be a looker" and "Attractive, smart, young, and no Catholics, or water signs." Finally, Democratic Representative James J. Delaney needed a temporary typist but demanded "White–no pantsuits." These prejudices from Democrats and Republicans are very telling. They reveal beliefs and biases about who should hold certain positions in a hierarchical congressional workplace. A 1977 House report found that Whites made up 88 percent of House workers and were overrepresented in higher salaried positions. In addition, although 57 percent of House employees were women, they were outnumbered by men in higher salaried positions by 10:1.[23]

In any other workplace these job ads would be illegal. This clear evidence of overt discrimination would prompt an investigation by the Equal Employment Opportunity Commission (EEOC), the agency Congress established in 1965 to enforce antidiscrimination law. Job seekers could also hold employers accountable for discrimination in the judicial system and receive a civil judgment. However, the Civil Rights Act of 1964, and as amended in 1972, did not cover congressional hiring practices and it did not allow for civil prosecution.

Title VII of the Civil Rights Act prohibits employment discrimination based on race, color, religion, sex, and national origin. However, the law did not apply to Congress or other parts of the federal government when it was originally passed. The term "employer" was defined as

> a person engaged in an industry affecting commerce who has twenty-five or more employees for each working day in each of twenty or more calendar weeks in the current or preceding calendar year, and any agent of such a person, but such term does not include (1) the United States, a corporation wholly owned by the Government of the United States, an Indian tribe, or a State or political subdivision thereof.

In 1972, Congress amended the law to include federal employees, providing them with the same rights as other workers, which included the ability to sue employers for discrimination.[24]

New Jersey Senator Harrison Williams remarked before voting on the amendment, "I am convinced that the language in the committee bill regarding Federal employees will prove a substantial help to those who, for so long, have been 'second class citizens,' as far as equal employment opportunity is concerned."[25] Specifically, the extension covered federal agencies and competitive jobs in the legislative and judicial branches, and the Library of Congress. California Senator Alan Cranston said the goal was not only to end federal exemption but also to make the federal government a "model employer of equal opportunity."[26] However, as lawmakers tried to make federal workplace laws more inclusive, they excluded one important group of workers, their own.

Members of Congress have exempted themselves from many federal workplace laws, including the National Labor Relations Act, National Fair Labor Standards Act, and the Occupational Safety and Health Act.[27] These laws gave workers the right to unionize, established a minimum wage and maximum number of work hours, and developed health and safety standards for workplaces. These laws are among the most important that Congress has ever passed. It put workers first and enshrined into law a basic level of well-being, decency, and equal treatment that should exist in the workplace. Why wouldn't Congress extend these basic rights to their own workers instead of treating them like second-class citizens?

Lawmakers have offered a few "practical" reasons why the law should not apply to them; however, these rationales, grounded in hypothetical worst-case scenarios, do not hold much weight. Rather, congressional exemption from federal workplace law is all about preserving lawmakers' power. At the core, "members feared placing themselves at the mercy of bureaucratic regulation that could limit their freedom to hire loyal, politically compatible staffers."[28] This "fear" crystallized in two different arguments. First, lawmakers argued that applying these laws to the legislature would violate the separation of powers between two coequal branches of the federal government. Since executive agencies monitor and enforce workplace law, this would mean executive oversight over Congress. Some argued this would produce a constitutional crisis. While there is certainly merit in protecting legislative prerogatives against executive branch encroachment, this does not mean that lawmakers could not still apply these rules and set up their own enforcement agency.

Second, another argument lawmakers used is that workplace laws were burdensome and prevented them from fulfilling their constitutional duties. They highlighted the particulars of being a political office holder, which required wide latitude and discretion, to recruit staff that they could trust and hire job candidates from their own constituencies. This belief still endures to this day. It is why congressional offices are run like "small businesses" and there is little oversight from congressional leadership and administrative units pertaining to personnel and office management.[29] However, even small businesses with fifteen or more employees follow federal workplace laws. Lawmakers could comply with federal law that promotes antidiscrimination and equal opportunity and hire compatible staff too. However, convincing lawmakers to give up some of their unlimited power in how they run their own offices and to follow workplace rules has proved extremely difficult.

In 1975, the House added Rule 43 to its official code of conduct, which provided that "a member, officer or employee of the House of Representatives shall not discharge or refuse to hire any individual, or otherwise discriminate against any individual with respect to compensation, terms, conditions, or privileges of employment, because of such individual's race, color, religion, sex, or national origin." Similarly, in 1977, the

Senate adopted Rule 50, which prohibited discrimination. The adoption of these rules allowed representatives and senators to signal their willingness to comply with the spirit of anti-discrimination law; however, enforcement of these principles proved a more difficult task.[30]

The adoption of these antidiscrimination rules is an example of symbolic compliance. While lawmakers passed these rules to show that they are not above the law, it is important to note that House and Senate rules do not have the same effect as federal law. There was no way to hold lawmakers accountable for violating these rules nor any mechanisms that would thwart this behavior in the first place. Edward Brooke, the only Black senator at the time, said, "Senate Rule 50 can only be viewed as a beginning. For, in essence, the Senate has now created a right for its employees but has not yet established procedures that would enable those employees to remedy violations of that right. And let us not deceive ourselves, 'a right without a remedy is like a bell without a clapper—hollow and empty.'"[31] It would take nearly twenty years from when lawmakers added nondiscrimination clauses to their codes of conduct for these principles to be codified in federal law and enforced.

During this intervening time a lot happened. Lawmakers contemplated various ideas about what enforcement might look like. Would they create an internal agency to review discrimination complaints? If they did, could they trust lawmakers to fairly review complaints against their peers, or should the agency be run by nonpartisan staff or even retired judges? Furthermore, would the agency have similar powers as the EEOC to review claims, or would it hold more robust power to root out racism and sexism as it existed throughout Capitol Hill? These questions were further complicated by Congress's own convoluted organizational structure, which is vast and decentralized. Congressional records show earnest attempts on behalf of some lawmakers to think through complicated questions about how to apply federal workplace laws to themselves. However, solving these problems should not have taken decades.

Change has been slow to come to Capitol Hill because legislative inequality does not get a lot of sustained public attention, and this ignorance allows lawmakers to offer symbolic compliance over structural change. As we will see, lawmakers have only willingly curbed their own power when they are confronted for practicing clear double standards. Highlighting this hypocrisy and the inequality it produced has been the strategy of congressional workers who suffer as second-class citizens, and in particular Black service workers, who are among the most affected by racism and sexism.

The Struggle Continues

Anne Walker was the general manager of the House restaurant system. She oversaw three large cafeterias, four carry-outs, two catering operations, and one full-service restaurant. After over a decade of service she was fired from her post in June 1982. She filed a lawsuit charging that her termination was based upon sexual discrimination. She alleged that Representative Ed Jones, the chairman of the House committee that oversaw the restaurant system, thought her $45,000 salary was "ridiculous for a woman." Representative Jones publicly stated that Walker had inefficient and improper bookkeeping practices and had skimmed funds.[32] This case was notable for numerous reasons. Lawmakers have long maintained that they should have complete discretion in executing their legislative work, including on personnel matters without interference from the executive and judicial branches. As we have learned, this is a key reason why lawmakers exempt themselves from antidiscrimination law, arguing it would violate the Speech and Debate Clause of the Constitution, which protects the legislative branch from judicial and executive encroachment. However, in this case, the court found there are limits to congressional immunity.

Appeals Court Judge Ruth Bader Ginsburg ruled that "personnel who attend to food service, medical care, physical fitness needs, parking, and haircutting for members of Congress no doubt contribute importantly to our legislators' well-being and promote their comfort and convenience in carrying out Article I business. But these staff members, unlike those who help prepare for hearings or assist in the composition of legislative measures, cater to human needs that are not 'intimately cognate to the legislative process.'" In this instance, the court recognized that the Speech and Debate Clause does not completely shield lawmakers from judicial inquiry and identified the rights of congressional service workers, albeit minimal, to seek redress. But for auxiliary workers like Ms. Walker, whose labor rights in the workplace were not guaranteed and clearly articulated, this was the beginning, not the end, of a decade-long struggle to achieve some of the basic rights that Congress has provided to all other workers.

Whereas the 1970s brought to public attention congressional exemption and discriminatory hiring practices in lawmakers' personal offices, the following decade demonstrated how this problem was much more pervasive and affected thousands of employees in auxiliary roles. A considerable amount of this activism came from congressional restaurants, where Ms. Walker worked. Cafeteria workers sought the right to unionize, which would allow them to engage in collective bargaining and establish a proper forum to address workplace grievances. Again, lawmakers exempted legislative branch employees from the National Labor Relations Act of 1935, which granted workers the right to join or form unions and protected them from employer retaliation for engaging in organizing efforts. The National Labor Relations Act is a pillar of federal workplace law that protects workers against discrimination and abuse and empowers them to negotiate for higher wages, better benefits, and other protections. This case further highlights legislative hypocrisy, and, more critically, reveals the real-life costs it has on ordinary Capitol Hill workers.

Cafeteria workers have long sought the right to unionize and bargain for higher wages in Congress.[33] Their movement gained traction in the late 1970s. In 1979, Senate cafeteria workers, who were mostly Black and Latino, formed the Capitol Employees Organizing Group. They wanted a union to address racist hiring and promotions. They were the most vocal group of congressional workers who used the plantation metaphor. Cafeteria workers grounded their own work experiences in historical discourses of racial exploitation to describe their position within the legislative hierarchy. For instance, restaurant workers who were employed in the Russell and Dirksen Senate office buildings referred to themselves as "field hands," while those who worked in more coveted positions in the Capitol were called "house niggers."[34] The field hands were among those who were fighting for unionization and alleged race-based promotions. Senate dining management was "angered" by the plantation metaphors, citing how in the Senate, workers earned $4.16 per hour, which was comparable or higher than wages in Washington-area restaurants. The plantation metaphor allowed union organizers to highlight racism in the management of the congressional restaurant system. Dorothy Garnett, who served as the treasurer of the union group, believed, "Whites come in and are moved up," while Black and Latino workers stayed put.

This could have been a straightforward problem that lawmakers solved—simply grant the restaurant workers who served them salads and sandwiches every day the right to unionize. During the early twentieth century, Congress took over managerial control of the various restaurants in the House, Senate, and Capitol buildings from private contractors to improve the quality of service and reduce costs.[35] This transition established cafeteria workers as legislative branch employees, entitling them to the privileges and immunities shared by other congressional personnel. The House and Senate each had their own committees that oversaw its restaurants while day-to-day operations were managed by the Architect of the Capitol, the federal agency responsible for the maintenance, operation, and preservation of the United States Capitol Complex. But this matter did not resolve itself quickly or easily. Instead, the movement unfolded in unexpected ways owing to a convoluted organizational structure that shared power between lawmakers, who were reluctant to address workers' complaints, and the Architect of the Capitol, who allegedly engaged in union-busting activities.

The union-organizing campaigns had different outcomes in the Senate and House. In the Senate, 60 percent of cafeteria workers signed cards indicating they wanted an independent union in 1980.[36] However, instead of recognition as a union, Senate cafeteria workers got the runaround from senators and congressional management. Part of the problem is that the organizational structure of Congress is anything but straightforward; it is complex and confusing. This confusion produces ambiguity about the rules and who has the decision-making power to change them. Jay Treadmill, the director of the Senate's three food operations, explained, "I work for the Architect of the Capitol, who works for the Senate and the Senate Rules Committee, which has jurisdiction over the Senate dining rooms. I am not opposed to the union, but, under the law, I have no authority to recognize one." However, the staff director of the Senate Rules Committee countered, "The architect of the Capitol is responsible for running the Senate dining rooms . . . The matter is not before the committee right now, and its best one unit, the architect deal with it." However, the Architect of the Capitol also refused to recognize the union. "Since we have no authority to deal with a union, it makes little sense to talk to an organization that calls itself one," said one Capitol administrator.[37]

Workers also made direct appeals to senators to no avail. In 1982, organizers appealed to the United Nations International Labor Organization to bring greater attention to their struggle and to shame lawmakers, who ironically were at the same time pressuring the Soviet Union and Poland to recognize union organizing efforts in their own countries. However, by the time the issue came before the Senate Rules Committee in 1983 and senators agreed to study the issue, 112 cafeteria workers signed petitions that they did not want a union.[38] Organizers intimated that their failure to sustain majority support was because congressional managers intimidated workers, suggesting that if they established a union, they would lose their jobs and the restaurant system would be privatized. Of course, in any other workplace these allegations would prompt scrutiny and investigations by the National Labor Relations Board. Similar allegations were made later when union-organizing efforts moved to the House.

Black and Latino cafeteria workers' union campaigns in the House centered on many of the same complaints as their Senate counterparts; however, the movement in the House produced a different outcome. In the House, cafeteria workers won the right to establish a union in 1987. This victory came at a cost. The House restaurant system was privatized, which effectively meant that cafeteria workers were no longer congressional employees and had the right to unionize.

This all began in 1984, when Democratic lawmakers transferred management of its restaurant system to the Architect of the Capitol. Two years later, a $776,000 surplus was gone, and the Architect declared that privatization was the best solution to fix a restaurant system that was not profitable and to recognize workers' rights. The changeover, which happened in 1987, coincided with a scheduled 3 percent raise for all federal workers. What's more, that same year, the salary of members of Congress rose from $75,100 to $89,500. However, because House restaurant workers were now employed by Service America Corporation, they did not get this adjustment.[39] Under their new contract, workers were allowed to keep their salaries and could not be fired for two years. Union organizers and a few Democratic representatives pointed out the obvious to anyone looking at this timeline, that privatization was retaliation for union organizing.

Representative William Lacy Clay took a leading role defending cafeteria workers. He argued that history was repeating itself in the House and alleged that the Architect of the Capitol was using the same antiunion activities it used in the Senate to stop unionization in the House. In an extended speech in 1986, Clay criticized his fellow Democrats for how they treated their lowest-paid and longest-serving employees:

> For over two years now, a majority of the employees in our cafeterias have petitioned for an election to vote on recognition and bargaining for a labor union. For over two years, every dilatory tactic in the book has been used to deny them this simple, just, legal right. Threats by management of job loss through contracting out, phony polls purporting to be elections conducted by the Architect and

cafeteria supervisors, arrest of union organizers, intimidation of those signing for the union.[40]

Clay provided affidavits by House employees who described confrontations with management over their participation in unionizing efforts, pointing out that if this had occurred in the private sector it would "be a very serious violation of law."

> "I was approached by a manager, Sally Crowe (Capitol Restaurant), who told me about the contracting out of the restaurant system. She said that this was being proposed because of the union effort and that if we stuck by the union, we would lose our jobs."

> "I have been harassed (by management) for wearing a union button."

> "I asked Odessa [assistant manager of the Longworth Cafeteria] if the rumor about contracting out of the restaurant system was true. Odessa said, 'Sure it is true—that's what your union got you.' She also said, 'What's more important—having a union or having your job?'"

> "Management acts like this is Russia—with spies running around and intimidation and all kinds of things."[41]

As dining workers made serious claims about workplace abuse from their supervisors, the Architect of the Capitol maintained that it did not have the power to collectively recognize House restaurant workers, as the office had stated years before in the Senate. However, legal experts on Capitol Hill concluded that was not true. The general counsel for the Speaker of the House found that "while the Architect's authority is presently limited by his role as an agent of the Committee, he could, nonetheless, adopt rules and regulations which would permit the formation of an employee association or union, and which would call for bargaining over the conditions of employment which are presently within the authority of the Architect to establish." This legal opinion was seconded by the Congressional Research Service. Ironically, while Democratic Speaker of the House Thomas O'Neill said that he supported unionization, he did little to settle this debate.[42]

A group of Democrats led by Representative Clay took to the House Floor to make this internal fight public. They questioned why Democratic leadership was so reluctant to grant unionization and pointed out how this was counter to the party's pro-worker values. Representative Barney Frank said, "The reason we are here is that the efforts that many of us made to deal with this in a conciliatory, informal way were rebuffed." His remarks discredited the prevailing and conservative argument that dining workers could not unionize due to the unique structure of Congress as a governing institution. "There are questions that are peculiar to us. That does not mean you should not allow people the fundamental right to vote to join unions. It means that you shape the right in that particular instance to take account of the peculiar institutional features."[43] To this end, one of the particulars of congressional restaurant work is nonstandard work schedules, which puts workers in a precarious labor position. California Representative Don Edwards explained, "The conditions under which the restaurant employees work are difficult ones. They have no effective grievance procedure. Many are laid off for recess periods and are forced to apply for unemployment compensation, which can take weeks or months to receive." They argued that unionization would allow restaurant workers to negotiate over the particulars of their work and be treated with dignity.[44] Representative Frank was "distressed" with his Democratic colleagues who professed pro-union sentiments but stood idly by and ignored workers in their own house. "It is about autonomy, it is about the right of individual working men and women to have some participation and not simply be ordered around."[45]

Legislative exemption did not just harm workers, it undermined the dignity of work more broadly. Representative Major Owens criticized the Architect's statement that unionization would be "extremely difficult and costly" and emphasized the dangers of this argument emanating from Congress. "It says also that unionization and collective bargaining is a radical idea, and if it gets going there is no telling where it will stop here on the Hill, and we must stamp out this radical idea among the restaurant employees before it gains any momentum and escalates. It is a sad document. I think it is sadder still that among Democrats in the Democratic Caucus that we have to debate the matter."[46] It is important to note that the Democrats' reluctance to champion and protect its own workers also coincided with the beginning of a neoliberal turn in government that saw public sector work privatized.[47]

The movement for unionization among congressional restaurant workers demonstrates a more complicated picture about how inequality persists on Capitol Hill. It captures how inequality is propelled by an organizational structure, where both federal workplace laws do not apply and there is ambiguity about the rules that do exist. Consequently, the absence of fair workplace rules on Capitol Hill enables those at the top of the congressional power structure to take advantage of those at the bottom, imposing significant economic and social harm. Relatedly, this case challenges our common understanding of how Congress works, and it raises important questions about who is actually in charge on Capitol Hill. Congress is large and decentralized. Representatives and senators have immense decision-making power, but so do a number of nonelected personnel across various offices and agencies.

However, the main reason why inequality in the congressional workplace festers is because lawmakers allow it. As Representative Clay declared when discussing the legality of whether dining workers could unionize, "What is lacking is the will, not the legal authority." Since the union movement began in 1979, House and Senate members both failed to act decisively. Lawmakers have a responsibility to thousands of workers that they directly and indirectly manage. To be a fair employer, lawmakers must follow the same rules they established for all other employers.

Abolishing the Last Plantation

In a rare moment of bipartisanship that almost seems unfathomable now, Republicans and Democrats banded together to end congressional exemption from federal workplace laws in 1995. The House of Representatives voted 390-0, and the Senate 98-1 to pass the Congressional Accountability Act. The law was simple: eleven already-existing federal workplace laws would be applied to Congress and its auxiliary agencies, like the Library of Congress and the Capitol Police. It established an independent, nonpartisan agency within the Capitol, the Office of Compliance, to enforce these provisions. Passage of the law was no easy feat; it took lawmakers years to build consensus on rules to apply federal workplace laws. As they voted on this legislation, lawmakers celebrated and proclaimed that they were abolishing the "last plantation." Republican Senator Charles Grassley, an author of the bill, was the most blunt: "Passage of the bill will mean that congressional employees will have the civil rights and social legislation that has ensured fair treatment of workers in the private sector." Grassley, who had worked on this issue for

the last several congresses, declared, "Congress is the last plantation. It is time for the plantation workers to be liberated!"[48]

Senator Grassley yielded the floor to Senator John Glenn,
who was a leading force behind the legislation. He had publicly admonished lawmakers for their hypocrisy and facilitated
a lot of the behind-the-scenes work, as well as the public hearings and the legislative analysis, which allowed Republicans
to act expeditiously once they assumed power in 1995 and
make the bill their first victory for the "Contract with America." Glenn testified, "My guiding principle has been that we
in Congress should be subject to the same laws as applied to
a business back in our home state."[49] He reminded his colleagues of the ire he drew being the first lawmaker to use
the plantation metaphor in 1978. The metaphor had been a
powerful rhetorical tool for him and others over the last two
decades, highlighting how Congress had excluded itself from
workplace rules that governed a new racial epoch, which featured a legal commitment to equal opportunity and antidiscrimination. Casting his vote on this milestone legislation, he
optimistically declared, "The last plantation, I think, we now
can eliminate and bring into the twentieth century with this
particular piece of legislation."[50]

In the preceding two decades, proponents of congressional workplace reform compiled evidence that supported the
plantation metaphor, illustrating a racial and gender hierarchy that placed White men in high-paid and influential roles
and constrained the careers of Black men, Black women, and
White women. While the plantation metaphor originally referenced Congress's exemption from federal workplace laws,
lawmakers, workers, and journalists later expanded upon the
metaphor to describe an unequal, racialized, and gendered
system of work inside the Capitol, an inequality regime. However, this attention to racial and gender inequality within the

congressional workplace disappeared when lawmakers passed the Congressional Accountability Act (CAA). Lawmakers received widespread adulation from journalists who hailed the legislation as a monumental triumph that constrained legislative power.[51] They had eliminated the last plantation, and thus—it seemed—there was no need to talk about inequality within the congressional halls any further. However, as we know, lawmakers did not stamp out racism and inequality in the congressional workplace.

While the CAA was an important milestone, ultimately the law did not go far enough to eliminate a systemic problem. For starters, the reason why people of color remain underrepresented in congressional staff positions is because compliance to federal workplace law alone is an insufficient tool to confront institutionalized inequality. Federal workplace law provides a legal framework to contest discrimination; it does not seek to proactively root out inequality. Consequently, the newly created Office of Compliance had limited influence over the management and administration of congressional offices.[52] Lawmakers did not personally commit to more inclusive and transparent hiring practices or ensuring that people of color occupy top staff positions in their personal offices or committees. If anything, the law legitimated insular hiring processes that yield persistent inequality. Additionally, representatives and senators did not offer better compensation and benefits to workers, which would help attract and retain a diverse workforce. In fact, lawmakers did the opposite. For more than two decades after the passage of the CAA, congressional office budgets declined, and wages remained stagnant.[53] In this way, the CAA is a symbolic shield that allowed lawmakers to signal compliance to federal workplace laws that promote antidiscrimination and equal opportunity and insulated them from further criticism.

When we look at what Congress did include in the CAA, we observe that the main problem with the law is that it did not live up to its name, it failed to hold lawmakers accountable. Lawmakers made bold assertions about how racism (and sexism) would no longer be an obstacle for congressional workers given the passage of this new law; however, they failed to provide the tools, either for themselves or for outsiders, to empirically assess if their efforts were successful. The law itself had a fatal flaw: it ignored the actual collection of data that would prove essential to gauge its effectiveness. Congress has never—and still does not—collect systematic demographic data (most obviously, race and gender) about its employees. Instead, the House and Senate contracted out this important to work to the Congressional Management Foundation, which conducts nonregular surveys on staff compensation and employment.[54] While these reports do provide information about the composition of the House and Senate staff, these data are based on surveys, which have variable response rates and do not yield complete systematic data. This lack of demographic information collected by Congress itself provides uncertainty to the exact racial and gender makeup of the congressional workplace. Moreover, this missing data makes it difficult to learn how positions are allocated, and to what extent racism and sexism might influence this process.

In other settings, these demographic data have been an invaluable tool for researchers to measure the presence of discrimination—it identifies if racial minorities can ascend to the highest levels of work in their organizations or if they are stunted. Put simply, these data help determine disparities in pay, promotion, and retention. Whereas employers are required by federal law to collect these data (and that collection is often a part of new employee onboarding) and report them to the Equal Employment Opportunity Commission, the absence of these data in Congress makes its actual functioning an enigma.

This lack of transparency also runs counter to the administration of the federal bureaucracy, which has publicly accessible information about how racial groups are employed in various departments and agencies. These data are clear and easy to understand. On the other hand, Congress reports its own employee information in ways that are difficult to study. The House and Senate each publish their own records, which list every paid employee's name, title, salary, and office. These records originally appeared in weighty tomes. The House now publishes their data as a CSV, which is easy to analyze. However, the Senate publishes their personnel data as a PDF, which can be between two thousand to three thousand pages long. Sorting through these data is labor intensive. It is like sorting through a large pile of encyclopedias to collect data on tens of thousands of workers and in which volumes are updated numerous times a year. What's more, since these data are compiled from individual offices, they are often filled with reporting errors, which only add to the length of time it takes to calculate an aggregated view of what the congressional workforce looks like. It should not be this hard to get a basic understanding of who works on Capitol Hill and to learn if these jobs are distributed equitably. This is an example of Congress saying it is transparent, but in reality, it is far from it. This lack of transparency is something that is repeated in the CAA and influences whether workers can individually and collectively hold lawmakers accountable.

The Congressional Accountability Act had other important faults, owing to how it was written and implemented. Lawmakers created a nontransparent disclosure process that shielded themselves from litigation brought by workers and reneged on allowing staffers to unionize. Fixing these failures has taken more than two decades. I focus on these two instances to show how reforming Congress is an ongoing process that relies on activism, and often public shame.

First, the CAA established a dispute resolution process for workers to bring claims against their bosses for workplace violations. Although this process was dramatically improved and streamlined in 2018, when lawmakers amended the CAA, I want to explain how this process initially worked and how it represented an instance of symbolic compliance. Imagine you worked on Capitol Hill, perhaps as a staff assistant. This was your dream job. While you love the work that you do, you do not like the way you are treated by your boss, who is a two-term representative. You believe this treatment is not only wrong, but it is harassment, a clear violation of the CAA. You weigh whether you should come forward with this because you know it will be a big deal. You work on Capitol Hill with some of the most powerful people in the country. They are worshiped as godlike figures on the Hill, and too often some of them act as if they are because they have been shielded from any type of punishment. What's more, stepping forward could have negative effects on your future career prospects in the House and Senate. Finally, you might even consider what this bad press might mean for your political party and the issues you care about. However, you decide it is important to come forward, so you approach the Office of Compliance to initiate a workplace harassment claim. What you discover is that this resolution process is drawn out and protects members of Congress more than it does you. Here is how it worked.

First, you would request counseling through the Office of Compliance. Next, the office would provide thirty days of counseling, which is then followed by thirty days of mandatory mediation with your employing office. If there is no resolution after these two months, you can proceed to the next step, which means either filing a formal complaint with the office or a lawsuit in Federal District Court, but not both. However, you can only reach this last step after you wait at least another thirty days, which is an unexplained requirement in the CAA. If you file a complaint with the Office of Compliance, your case will be heard and decided by an outside third party who has the power to award a monetary settlement.[55]

As you go through this process, you notice several flaws in the Congressional Accountability Act. First is the mandatory mediation rule. Federal workplace law does not require mediation for most federal or private sector employees who bring harassment complaints. In other parts of the federal government, an employee has forty-five days after an incident of workplace harassment to file a claim with the Equal Employment Opportunity Commission (EEOC). After the complaint, the EEOC has 180 days to investigate the claim and offer a resolution. Second, on Capitol Hill, during mandatory mediation, you as an employee are not provided with any type of legal counsel; however, your office is represented by the Office of House Employment Counsel.[56] As you might imagine, this type of arrangement creates an imbalance of power, which provides protection for lawmakers and Congress as an institution rather than accusers. Third, you would think that this lengthy process would mean an investigation into the alleged violations, but the CAA did not authorize the Office of Compliance to investigate claims. Fourth, the money you receive as a settlement comes from an account in the Treasury department appropriated by Congress and funded by taxpayers, not the representative. Lawmakers structured the law to hold employing offices accountable, not themselves. This decision, as legal scholar James Brudney notes, "immunizes members from personal liability" and reversed a previous standard by which representatives and senators were financially responsible for unlawful behavior.[57] Finally, this whole process is cloaked in secrecy and requires little disclosure. During mediation, all parties sign a confidentiality agreement, and that same confidentiality applies for any potential settlement. The public knows little about how it has paid a settlement for egregious behavior and how it continues to pay the salary of an accused lawmaker.[58] This is how the process worked for over two decades.

In another clear example of Congress saying one thing and doing another, taxpayers paid over $17 million to settle various workplace claims between 1995–2017. Though lawmakers said this was a form of accountability, it is unclear to whom they were accountable. Details about these settlements were, until very recently, secret. Congress did not initially report the number of settlements or the total amount paid each year. Furthermore, the public was not provided with any details about these cases, including what the settlements are for and who is accused. Lawmakers instituted a rule to hold themselves accountable but then did not live up to the spirit of the law.[59]

Congress's culture of unaccountability changed after a series of high-profile scandals involving lawmakers and top staffers took place amid a global reckoning with sexism. In 2006, Representative Mark Foley resigned in disgrace after harassing Senate pages. Four years later, Representative Eric Massa admitted to inappropriate behavior with his staff and left Capitol Hill. This led to an $85,000 settlement paid by taxpayers.[60] That same year, Representative Mark Souder resigned after it became known he had an affair with one of his staffers. That same scenario played out again the following year with Senator John Ensign.[61] In 2014, Lauren Greene sued her boss Representative Blake Farenthold for sexual harassment and gender discrimination in Federal District Court. She said another aide told her that their boss confided to him that he had sexual fantasies about Greene. She also shared that the congressman said to her that he had not sex with his wife for years. In court, she alleged she was inappropriately fired. The case was settled with a $84,000 payment to Greene paid by US taxpayers. Details of this case only became known a few years later as the #MeToo movement began, spreading from Hollywood to Washington, DC.[62] Again, the Office of Compliance said it could not reveal many details about the case because it would violate its confidentiality agreements.

The #MeToo movement propelled a global reckoning with sexual harassment and motivated millions to speak out about wrongs in their workplace, including on Capitol Hill. Among those speaking out was Representative Jackie Speier, who said when she was a young Hill staffer in her early twenties, her chief of staff held her face and forcibly kissed her. Speier encouraged other victims to speak out and break the Hill's culture of silence by sharing on social media under #MeTooCongress.

Harassment is an underreported problem on Capitol Hill, especially for those employed directly by lawmakers. In a survey of congressional staff by *CQ* and *Roll Call*, four in ten women believed sexual harassment was a problem on the Hill, and one in six said they had been personally victimized.[63] Most astonishingly, nine out of ten staffers were unaware of the Office of Compliance, the agency Congress created to tackle this very problem. Given how the law was written, we should not be too surprised that harassment continued on the Hill after the passage of the CAA and that the workers did not know how to report it. Speier described the resolution process as more "institution-protection" rather than "victim-friendly."[64] As she points out, had the accountability law been written to actually encourage transparency, that might have created another problem for lawmakers: "I think we would find that sexual harassment is rampant in the institution.

But no one wants to know, because they'd have to do something about it."[65] To this end, in 2017, over a thousand former congressional staffers signed a letter demanding lawmakers reform the CAA.[66]

Led by women lawmakers, Congress amended the Congressional Accountability Act in 2018 to provide greater transparency and ease workers' burdens. Under the new CAA Reform Act, workers are provided with a confidential advisor to assist them and a shortened administrative process that waives mandatory mediation. In addition, lawmakers are now personally responsible for paying any harassment settlements.[67] Finally, the Office of Compliance, renamed as the Office of Congressional Workplace Rights, provides more data about cases and settlements on its website.

Finally, another way that lawmakers continued to not live up to the principles they preached involves congressional staff unionization. As we have learned with food service workers, congressional employees had for decades almost no bargaining power over their salaries, benefits, or working conditions. However, in almost all other work settings, employees can unionize to advocate for themselves. Congress partially ended this double standard with the CAA. The law allowed some legislative branch employees to unionize, namely workers in the Capitol Police and Government Accountability Office. Moreover, the law then tasked the Office of Compliance with studying if it was feasible to allow congressional staff employed in personal, leadership, committee, and support offices to unionize and how this process would work. The law required the Office of Compliance to study this issue and promulgate rules.

As Demand Progress reports, "To the surprise of House leadership, a majority of the OOC board members found that no exceptions were necessary and that congressional staff should be permitted to unionize under similar rules as the

Executive Branch, and promulgated regulations setting forth how this process would work."[68] To adopt these regulations, lawmakers only had to pass a simple resolution in the House and Senate to cover their respective employees, and a joint resolution to cover all remaining employees. That's it. House Republicans rejected the Office of Compliance's rules, and House Democrats never took up the issue.[69] Senator Charles Grassley, an author of the CAA, lamented the impasse: "This is a disgrace to the principles supporting the CAA. Congress has not approved these regulations because a number of powerful members disagree with their content."[70]

It took over twenty-five years for lawmakers to finally allow (at least some) staffers to unionize. Many different actors contributed to this effort, which provides an instructive model for what it takes to hold Congress accountable. Demand Progress, a nonprofit that focuses on strengthening congressional capacity and increasing legislative transparency, helped jumpstart the contemporary congressional staff unionization movement. They brought the issue back to the forefront by writing white papers and providing expert testimony that explained the existing rules on unionization and what lawmakers needed to do to permit staffers to unionize.[71] Their research and advocacy laid the groundwork for a larger social movement, built on staffers' discontent, to seize this issue.

In early 2022, @dear_White_staffers, an anonymous Instagram account, began posting about rampant racism, sexism, and workplace abuses on Capitol Hill.[72] The account featured unnamed submissions from countless congressional staffers that demonstrated a clear and pervasive toxic workplace environment. One of the key demands was the right to unionize, which was expressed amid a renewed interest in union membership nationwide. In February 2022, Pablo Manríquez, a reporter for *Latino Rebels*, asked Speaker of the

House Nancy Pelosi if she supported the right of congressional staff to unionize. She replied rather matter-of-factly, "Well, we just unionized at the DCCC (Democratic Congressional Campaign Committee), and I supported that."[73] Within a few hours her office released a press statement with a clearer and stronger endorsement of congressional staff unionization. On the surface the Speaker's response might be what you would expect from a Democrat. However, her response was surprising and newsworthy because she had done little to advance congressional staff unionization during either of her two stints as Speaker up until now. Pelosi's powerful endorsement propelled the Congressional Workers Union, a newly formed group of staffers fighting for the ability to unionize. Within three months, House Democrats passed a resolution allowing House staff to unionize and fulfilled a promise twenty-five years overdue.[74]

In the House, unionization happens office by office, depending upon a majority vote of office staff. In September 2022, staff in Representative Andy Levin's office became the first office to unionize.[75] A month later, this union negotiated a $10,000 raise for its staffers.[76] Staff unionization continues at a slow pace in the House and, so far, has survived a Republican attempt to nullify union-organizing rules.[77]

Senate staffers are still not permitted to unionize. The majority of senators, in both parties, have so far refused to support legislation giving Senate staff the right to unionize. Technically, Senate offices can still unionize, but if they did, they would not have the protections of federal labor law that prevents retaliation against organizing. In addition, senators can individually choose to recognize a union in their office. In March 2023, Senator Ed Markey became the first senator to recognize their Senate staff as a union.[78]

These movements tell us something we have learned before: lawmakers act when they are held accountable. This might sound easy, but it is not. The organization and management of the congressional workplace is so opaque, and a strong culture of not speaking out helps strengthen Congress as an inequality regime. This opaqueness makes it difficult to learn about the full scope of how inequality is institutionalized on the Hill. Without transparency it is difficult to hold lawmakers accountable.

A Model Employer

Most Americans disapprove of Congress as an institution—a trend that has only intensified over time.[79] Part of this disapproval is because the legislative branch is dysfunctional—Congress cannot seem to get anything done. Another major influence is that lawmakers do not do what they say. They make promises to voters that they do not fulfill, and as this chapter has shown they make rules they do not follow.

In a hearing in the 1980s to apply civil rights laws to the Senate, Senator John Glenn explained that this congressional double standard does great damage to the public's perception of Congress and likened it to "a doctor prescribing medicine for a patient that he himself would not take."[80] At the same hearing, Republican Senator John Heinz, another proponent of congressional reform, offered another example: the legislature was like a lawless country that operated under the assumption, "For my friends, anything; for my enemies, the law." By not following the law, Heinz argued that lawmakers defied the expectations of the Founding Fathers, like James Madison, who wrote that Congress should "make no law which will not have its full operation on themselves and their friends as well as on the great mass of society."[81] When lawmakers do not follow the rules it erodes public trust in Congress, and it also harms tens of thousands of workers on Capitol Hill.

The Congressional Accountability Act applied federal work-place laws to Congress and reversed a decades-long standard of congressional exemption. But as we have learned, the law had serious flaws and did not go far enough. Importantly, the law did not include the necessary tools to hold lawmakers accountable. Demographic data, antiharassment protocols, and unionization are all crucial tools to hold lawmakers accountable to the law.

It goes without saying that I think lawmakers should follow all federal workplace rules, but even that sets the bar too low. As nationally elected leaders, lawmakers should lead by example. Reforming the congressional workplace is an opportunity for lawmakers to model democratic principles and what it means to be a good employer. It is also a chance to improve the legislature's negative reputation. Crucial to being a good employer means treating your employees with respect. What proponents of the plantation metaphor argued is that the exemption from the law empowered lawmakers to act with impunity, often at the expense of Hill workers' dignity.

CHAPTER TWO

Climbing the Hill

THE BURDEN OF RACE, CLASS, AND SOCIAL NETWORKS

Blacks are totally excluded from these hidden decision-making networks, irrespective of how many Blacks we might elect. This is a system that has its roots in exclusive White schools, clubs, neighborhoods, political groups, and so forth. It is a self-reinforcing form of institutionalized racism.

—REGINALD GILLIAM, AFRICAN AMERICAN
AIDE TO SENATOR JOHN GLENN, 1978[1]

That's why Congress is sometimes referred to as "the last plantation." Congress simply doesn't have to abide by antidiscrimination laws in hiring. Attempts to enforce antidiscrimination rules on congressmen are regularly beaten down. Discrimination complaints theoretically can go to the ethics committees, but the procedures involved and the fear of retribution make the route difficult.

—VERNON JORDAN, AMERICAN BUSINESSMAN
AND CIVIL RIGHTS ACTIVIST, 1979[2]

MICHELLE IS ONE the highest ranking and most influential Black political professionals in the twenty-first century. She has worked for top Democrats in the House, Senate, and White House. Her career in Washington politics began on Capitol Hill in the 1990s. Getting onto the Hill, as she described it, was extremely hard, but also very simple: it was determined in part by relationships and in part by luck. In her case, she relied on the assistance of a law school mentor, a Black man, to navigate a nontransparent congressional job market, which landed her a job working as counsel on a House subcommittee. "It really was a mixture of that network of talking to someone via the law school, with huge relationships with people on the committee because of the civil rights work that he did, and an opening being there that hadn't been there in quite some time."

Committee jobs are hard positions to get, in part because they are occupied by policy and legal experts; thus, they tend to have less turnover than a lawmaker's personal office, where staffers are more likely to be generalists and stay for shorter periods. When Michelle reached out to the subcommittee through her mentor's help, they told her of an open spot for assistant counsel in their office, which they hadn't had in almost a decade. After interviewing with the subcommittee staff and the chairman, she got the job.

As Michelle gained seniority and became a top staffer in the Senate, she obtained an aerial view of how the congressional workplace as a whole operated. She saw, over and over again, different manifestations of the same thing: an opaque hiring process that perpetuated inequality and limited the number of people of color working on the Hill. This view from the top allowed her to see how her experience was, unfortunately, far from unique.

Congress is a black box. It's a hard place . . . that you can't really see in, and it's hard for us to figure out how to get in. But once you're there it's easier to navigate and to move around and to see new jobs and to be recommended for new jobs. And I think all of that makes it a more challenging place, particularly when you're thinking about diversity issues.

Getting on the Hill is an incredibly difficult process that relies, as Michelle points out, on knowing the right person. Knowing the right person helps demystify the hiring process, which features over 535 personal offices and dozens of committee offices. If you know someone on the inside, she explained, they can inform you (before the information is shared with the general public) of which jobs are available, how best to apply, and who to contact in the office to learn more about the open position. If they like you, they can even move your resume from the bottom of the stack to the top.

But "knowing the right person" is not always in your control—it's determined by who your parents are, where you grew up and attended school, what type of previous work experiences you have had, and how savvy you are at social networking from these privileged locations. One Black Senate staffer put it this way, "The Hill is an almost incestuous place. You have to know someone, and that person has to have pull." If this does not seem fair to you, you are right. It's not. Again and again, the job search process on Capitol Hill ends up as an insider's game, which benefits not the best candidate for the job, but the most well-connected and best-informed candidate.

In this chapter, I demonstrate how Black professionals gain access to a notoriously nontransparent and insular institution. To make it inside they need help, a guide to help them navigate the black box that Michelle described. The job search process is a social process—70 percent of Black staffers I interviewed got their first job after interning or through someone they knew. Social networks help Black staffers maneuver through the informality of the congressional job market—by which there is no standardized system to recruit and hire job seekers—and navigate its opaqueness and the uncertainty and frustration that comes with it.

I focus on three pathways into the congressional workplace and explain how institutional, racial, and economic barriers shape who gets hired. First, I focus on the difficulties of directly applying for a job with no assistance. While not impossible, this path is arduous and rare, because of the federal legislature's decentralized organizational structure. Additionally, staffers who are responsible for hiring are given little training and support to do so. As a result, this gives rise to insular and exclusionary hiring processes.

Second, congressional internships provide an opportunity to learn how the legislature works up close; they also socialize and prepare newcomers for paid staff positions on the Hill. However, for the last few decades, the overwhelming majority of congressional internships were unpaid. This meant that, to get your foot in the door, you had to work for free or secure one of the few paid intern positions.[3] Some interns value working in the legislative branch so much that they have worked a second job to subsidize their unpaid internship, while others have taken out loans to cover their living expenses. Programs like the Congressional Black Caucus Foundation, which provides stipends and housing for a few dozen Black students each year, have been instrumental. However, these programs cannot afford to compensate the thousands of students who come to the Hill each year. As a result, these economic preconditions set the stage for an unrepresentative class of interns, which, subsequently, creates and perpetuates a racially stratified legislature.

Third, I examine how social encounters facilitated by family, friends, and acquaintances lead to getting hired. Here Black staffers recount their stories of being helped through congressional insiders. However, the same social forces that give Black professionals access are the same that make Congress racially exclusive.

Capitol Hill is a space dominated by White lawmakers and White staffers. Their overrepresentation coupled with informal and insular hiring practices allow Whites to hoard job opportunities.[4] Whereas in the previous chapter I illustrated how exemption from federal workplace law created a foundation for a racially stratified legislative workplace to exist, here I show how this inequality regime is reproduced through hiring. I use Black staffers' paths to Congress, which vary in difficulty, to describe a dysfunctional hiring process and to pinpoint how existing racial and economic inequality intersect and become amplified in the political sphere.

Applying Isn't Straightforward

Audrey described her entrée to the Hill as lucky; her path is an exceedingly rare one. "Nobody referred my resume," she told me. She did not have any type of in with the office or Congress at large. "A lot of people have, 'Hey, I have a friend who's referring you in or I know the member, or I know somebody on the Hill,' but at the time, I wasn't that person." She sent in her application blind. She remembered reading a job announcement for a legislative assistant with a policy portfolio that included civil rights and criminal law as well as product liability and copyrights. She was intrigued by the job description and applied. This was one of the first congressional job announcements she read, and the only staff position she applied to. "Just by luck and good timing, I was able to get an

interview and it went pretty well, I guess, because I was hired."
Audrey was one of the few people I interviewed who entered
the notoriously insular legislative workplace with no assistance
and overall ease. However, for most people with no connections
to Congress, finding a job on Capitol Hill is confusing. Really,
really confusing.

Imagine that you just graduated college. You are determined to move to Washington, DC, and get a job on the Hill.
You don't know anyone who works there already. So, you do a
google search or you may even ask your favorite political science professor for advice. You discover there are two central
job boards online, the House and Senate employment bulle-
tins. They separately list vacancies for each chamber. The lists
can be quite massive. You are a bit bewildered. They adver-
tise all available positions, even vacancies for service jobs. You
search for the job you want, an aide to a senator, but there is
no search box at all, so you sift through each ad hoping not
to miss the one that is right for you. After you sort through
this unedited list, you apply to a few, but you never hear back.
Later, you'll learn that those jobs have already been shared,
weeks earlier, through the social networks of existing staffers. The positions were probably filled before they were even
listed on the job board.

As you do more research, you discover that it is surprisingly
difficult to apply to jobs in Congress. The House and Senate
both have resume banks, where applicants can upload their
resume each quarter. Additionally, the House is a little more
technologically advanced—it allows applicants to apply for
fourteen different job titles. If you click the right title, your
resume can even be viewed, without much work from you, by
offices looking to hire for those specific positions. But getting
a job on the Hill more often means directly applying to each
office and often using informal methods.

What you have discovered through the job search process is that although we are taught that Congress is a singular institution, in reality it functions as a highly decentralized work organization made up of hundreds of offices. There are 535 personal offices and nearly fifty committees and even more subcommittees. All have their own application process. There are also congressional leadership offices and congressional caucuses. Not only do you have to apply individually to offices, the process looks differently from one office to another. You apply to one office with a resume and cover letter, but another office asks for writing samples. Each office also has their own hiring criteria. This adds to your burden. You're exhausted and overwhelmed. The entire process can feel frustrating and chaotic. That's because it is. Finding and sorting through this information is in itself a job. Maybe you had thought or hoped, starry-eyed, that an institution as important and powerful as the federal legislature would have a more organized hiring process. It does not.

In elite industries, from law to finance to business, employers invest significant monetary and human resources to find the best talent, visiting students at campus job fairs and conferences to make their pitch and provide information about the hiring process. Of course, these elite employers say they want the best talent, but then they recruit from an inherently small pool, prioritizing predominantly White institutions and using criteria that favors hiring students from economically privileged backgrounds. Their process is inherently exclusionary.[5]

Congress is just as exclusionary as other elite workplaces. Lawmakers do not actively and openly recruit for staffers. Instead, they rely on the allure of working on Capitol Hill and expect applicants to come to them. This establishes Congress as what Alexander Furnas and Tim LaPira call a seller's market, where lawmakers (and their staff) have all the power and no incentive to change.[6]

Since each office establishes their own hiring protocols, it creates a system of disorganization that is not easily navigable or transparent. As a consequence of this decentralization, the congressional workplace lacks professionalization, meaning it has not developed large-scale efficiencies to deal with knotty problems like hiring and how to make the entire process fair and inclusive. Some offices are better than others; they may put in place a well-organized system to collect, manage, and evaluate applications. However, for many offices the submission system is as simple as sending your resume and cover letter to a generic Gmail address. You may wonder if your application was received and evaluated or lost and unseen.

Furthermore, the people who oversee the hiring process are just the senior staffers in that particular office. They lack any professional training in human resources, and they do not have the support of a human resources department. In the House, Democrats, recently created the Office of Diversity and Inclusion, which has done extensive work to recruit, prepare, and recommend qualified job candidates. However, nonpartisan offices like this are relatively disempowered and have almost no influence in the management of individual offices.[7] Senior staffers must sort through dozens, and sometimes hundreds, of applications on their own. This process lacks any internal evaluation to measure racial and gender disparities and mitigate bias. From this lack of professional training and coordination, staffers who are already overworked and overwhelmed turn to insular and quick-fix methods (often nepotistic and exclusionary), like recruiting peers and close contacts to ease the burden of a demanding job.[8] Consequently, what lawmakers see when they interview finalists and ultimately hire a job candidate is the result of a skewed process. This lack of transparency and decentralization is what makes finding a job in the congressional workplace like navigating within a black box, and, importantly, it is what establishes it as an inequality regime.

Information about openings for paid staff positions is not openly shared, at least not at first, which means that, if you are an outsider, directly applying for positions can be confusing, difficult, and time-intensive. However, the opposite is true about internships. That is, every congressional office hires interns and promotes these routine openings according to the undergraduate semester schedule (fall, spring, and summer). This information is a standard feature on the websites of members of congress and sometimes shared through colleges and universities' career services listservs. This pathway into Congress is more straightforward and perhaps less daunting; however, that does not mean this route is without barriers.

The Intern Pipeline

Keisha was a legislative assistant for a White Republican senator, and Deidre was the legislative counsel for a White Democratic representative. Despite their differences in political affiliation, Keisha and Deidre had a lot in common. They were both Black attorneys who secured their first full-time jobs on the Hill through congressional internships. In college, Keisha interned for a representative and then returned to work for him after she graduated from law school and he became a senator. Deidre, however, became a congressional intern after she obtained her law degree. Even with an elite credential, she discovered that becoming a postgraduate intern was the only way she could develop the social contacts necessary to advance through the insular hiring practices on Capitol Hill. Their career journeys demonstrate the crucial import of internships as a gateway to congressional careers. Their pathways are not wholly unique. A recent survey of congressional staff showed that over 50 percent of staffers started their careers on Capitol Hill as interns.[9] However, Keisha and Deidre did stand out in one way: the overwhelming majority of congressional interns are White.[10] Keisha and Deidre's pathways, as additional exceptions to the rule, demonstrate why this is the case.

Interning on the Hill is an age-old tradition that goes back decades. An estimated six thousand men and women, mostly undergraduates, travel annually to Capitol Hill to intern.[11] All congressional offices take advantage of this excess supply of labor as they recruit, screen, and hire interns. Most interns work directly for lawmakers in their personal offices in DC, and some work in state district offices. There are also internship opportunities in congressional committees and leadership offices, which are more prestigious and competitive. It is not uncommon for students to intern more than once and for them to use their past work experience to ladder up to better internships.

The high season is the summer, when most college students are not enrolled in any classes and look for employment. As the notoriously hot and humid Washington summer approaches, House offices hire a handful of interns and squeeze them into their already tight working quarters. In the Senate, where offices have much more square footage and spacious accommodations, there can be dozens of interns working together during the summer months. The Capitol hallways transform and brim with these young and eager new faces. Over the course of several weeks, they receive a crash course in how Congress works that includes the basics of lawmaking and navigating its labyrinthine structure.

For Keisha, the idea of interning on Capitol Hill came at the suggestion of a dean in college who thought it would be a good fit for her political interests and knew that a local congressman was looking for interns. She landed an internship with a

White Republican, who at the time was a House member and representative for her parents' district. Her lawmaker offered Keisha a paid internship, which at the time was very rare.

For the last thirty years, interning on the Hill meant working for free. Thousands upon thousands of students, who worked full-time hours in the summer or part-time in the fall and spring, were offered academic credit rather than a salary. These internships were marketed as priceless experiences that allowed students to learn about legislative power and relish in it. What's more, these unpaid internships have been legitimated by a broader neoliberal ideology that tells workers that working for free is a part of the dues they must pay to get a good job.[12] But interning with no compensation wasn't always the case.

When the Hill internship program took off in the postwar period, Congress allocated a significant budget for offices to pay interns. For example, Sahil Desai found that in 1971 almost all House offices offered paid internships. When Lyndon B. Johnson died in 1973, lawmakers honored the late president, who previously served in the House and Senate, by naming its internship program after him. "Each House office was given money to hire interns in two-month stints who would be paid $500 per month, a stipend that was routinely raised to match inflation, and which today would amount to around $2,700."[13] Intern compensation was equivalent to what a staff assistant might make today. While individual offices still oversaw their own internship program, the collective decision by lawmakers to provide dedicated funding is important. This institution-wide program, named after a president, no less, identified the value of paying interns a dignified wage and its civic dividends for our representative democracy. The paid program opened the doors of Congress to train a new generation of public leaders from a variety of backgrounds. Unfortunately, a narrower and more neoliberal mindset aimed at shrinking the size of government and reducing federal spending took over Washington in the 1990s and effectively eliminated paid internships. As you might imagine, the rise of unpaid internships closed the door for many students from marginalized and less affluent backgrounds to work in Congress for a few months, but the costs have been even greater. Internships help launch political careers, and reducing access to this crucial and formative entry point to the congressional workplace has clear long-term consequences for who gets to hold positions of power.

Before Keisha started her internship in the early 2000s, she thought that "interns were nothing more than glorified coffee getters." Her perception was not necessarily wrong. Internships can be hit or miss. Some offices train students to learn the intimate, inner workings of Congress; others use interns as unofficial office assistants, to answer the phone, give tours, and respond to large piles of constituent mail. This wide variation in internship quality is a byproduct of the decentralization of Congress, where there is no institutional guidance that defines internship goals or what skills students should acquire. She described the uneven training and support interns receive in this way:

> There is really no hand-holding through the internship process. There is no formal process of how someone is introduced. Each office has their own way of orienting their interns to the Hill. Some offices will do hand-holding, but others are sink or swim. It depends on the congressman, and it also depends on the culture within their mini office. Each office would give someone a totally different experience.

Keisha lucked out—she landed in a supportive office and found a legislative assistant (LA) who become her mentor. She described herself as a nag as she approached the LA, a

White woman who was pregnant, and offered to help reduce her workload. She remembered saying to the LA, "You must need some help; you're tired, you're seven months pregnant. I know there is something I can do for you." Her persistence paid off in more ways than one. Not only did she gain more substantive work responsibilities as an intern, but these few months were important training for the work she would later do in her career. Explaining the connection, she said:

> She was working on judiciary and budget issues. She just ended up assigning me to a reentry project she was working on with another congressman. I did a lot of tracking back and forth and looking at the different memos and making sure each office had the correct information while she was trying to draft a bill. Lo and behold, when I actually worked in the Senate I ended up working on the same issue that I'd helped with while I was an intern.

This experience helped build her expertise on legislative issues and, more critically, provided firsthand instruction on what congressional staff do. As she mentioned, congressional offices provide little support in terms of professional development. Therefore, because of the informal organization of congressional offices, an important way that congressional staffers learn their jobs is by watching others and talking to them about their work.

> I really spent time talking to people that had the entry-level positions inside of the office to see what their days were like and how they were adapting to DC, to see if that was something that I wanted to do. When I talked to them, the culture and the environment in the office was fine; they did point out that it was a lot of work. Depending on who your congressman was you could have someone who has

the personality who is more hands-off and gives a lot of breadth and authority to their legislative aides, assistants, and on down the line, and it leads to a lot of innovation, or you can have an office where someone is more hands-on and so they want to see everything before it goes out, they want to be sure they've reviewed everything.

Keisha's office observations were astute. Not only did she observe what her coworkers did, but she began to notice who held influence in the office. These observations allowed her to understand congressional office hierarchies and how to navigate this system as a Black woman. After her internship, Keisha declined a job offer to be a staff assistant in the office. Given her experiences, she knew that this junior position lacked influence and power. She also knew that this public-facing role could easily transform into a racialized role. And she refused to be used to deflect allegations of racism within the Republican Party.

Instead, Keisha went to law school. During this period, she stayed in contact with her lawmaker and his chief of staff. She sent them quarterly updates that included details about how she was doing in school and photos of herself to make them remember her face. "I always stayed in contact with his chief of staff. I was just like, 'Yeah, I know you offered me a job, but I didn't want it, thank you. I ain't gonna be your Black face,'" she said with a laugh. As a reward for her frequent correspondence, the office invited her to special events whenever the congressman returned home. "Every time we would see each other he would take time out just to say, 'How are you?'" she said. "People love to brag on folks, 'This was one of my interns and she decided to turn down a job and go to law school. Who does she think she is?' It always made him look good anyway."

Her years-long relationship with her lawmaker and his senior staff positioned her to get a job with him after she graduated law school and he became a senator. Moreover, it was this relationship that she leveraged to get the right position. She explained:

> I knew I wanted to come back in a different capacity. After being on the Hill for several months as an intern you might not know what the legislative assistant is doing but you know that person is spending more time with the actual senators or congressmen, and they are doing something where they are persuading him to have a particular position. I knew that if I came back to the Hill that I would have to be in a position that would give me access to my senator. Also, I had to have an issue that he had a vested interest in. If your senator doesn't like the budget and you're the budget person, you won't have that face-to-face time and you won't have an issue where you and he will actually have true conversations and correspondence.

Here Keisha elaborates on a key point that she mentioned earlier—that she benefited from knowing the difference between staff positions and how they each fit within office hierarchies. This insight influenced her negotiations during the hiring process. First, the new senator hired her directly, bypassing the traditional hiring process by which the legislator's senior staff would screen all candidates and then recommend a few, from which the legislator would choose (although oftentimes they simply follow the recommendation their staff). However, when she subsequently spoke to the chief of staff, he offered her a role as a legislative correspondent. The latter position is more junior and constrains a staffer to a more passive role conducting research and writing legislative correspondence. Legislative assistants, however, brief lawmakers on votes and hearings and have a more active role. "I told the chief of staff, 'You must be out your damn mind. I'm going to talk to the senator about that.'" She met with the senator in his state office and told him, "You want me to be an LA, right?" As she tells it, he replied, "Sure. I wouldn't expect you to be a legislative correspondent, you just graduated from law school." This direct negotiation with a lawmaker probably would not have happened if Keisha did not have a personal relationship with him. In normal instances a senior staffer's recommendation would be final.

Keisha's experience demonstrates the multilayered reasons why congressional internships are pivotal in assisting former interns get jobs in Congress. These opportunities and the relationships that develop from them help interns secure more desirable positions that offer greater influence and mobility. Keisha's experience provided her with on-the-ground training for the legislative issues that she would work on directly a few years later. It also gave her insider status. She knew her lawmaker and his key advisors, and they all knew her. She was deliberate in making sure they all remembered her after she left the office. Keeping in touch reflected how genuinely appreciative she was of the opportunity and was also a savvy strategy. At the same time, cultivating these relationships allowed her to tackle the elephant in the room, race. The personal relationship she had with her lawmaker not only allowed her to discuss her desired role, but it also enabled her to discuss the obvious: she was a Black woman working for a White Republican. In the same meeting she negotiated to be a legislative assistant over a more junior role, she told her lawmaker, "I don't want to be your front face. I don't want to be your Black face." He assured her she would not be racialized in her work. In the next chapter, we will see how Keisha used her personal relationships, seniority, and expertise to challenge racism in policymaking.

Importantly, Keisha was able to have this experience because she was paid. She quipped, "I didn't have an issue with asking and he did not have a problem with providing." However, most people who intern on Capitol Hill are not paid. According to analysis from Pay Our Interns, in 2017 only 10 percent of congressional offices offered paid internships.[14] Therefore to work as a congressional intern a student had to find one of the few offices that offered compensation, or apply for support from an external organization, or work for free. By and large, most internships offer no support and there are not enough organizations to supplement the vast number of unpaid internships. The takeaway from this type of employment system is clear: it advantages students from affluent backgrounds. They are the ones who can afford to work for free for several months in an expensive city like Washington, DC. For everyone else, this important entry point to Congress is inaccessible. Due to systemic racism in the United States, affluence is highly correlated with Whiteness, and therefore this system systematically excludes those who are non-White.

In 2018, Congress took a major step toward removing these economic barriers for accessing congressional employment and passed legislation to fund paid internships.[15] Initially, the law provided each House office with $20,000 and Senate offices with upward of $50,000, depending on the size of its state population, to pay interns. I reviewed payroll data from the first year this new program was implemented.[16] I found that White students were disproportionately overrepresented among paid interns while Black and Latino students were underrepresented.[17] For example, White students make up only 52 percent of the national undergraduate population but accounted for 76 percent of paid interns. On the other hand, Black and Latino students make up 15 and 20 percent of the undergraduate population but accounted for 7 and 8 percent of paid interns, respectively.[18] Adding to these racial inequalities, lawmakers disproportionately hired students from private universities for paid internships. Although 26 percent of undergraduates nationally attend private universities, 48 percent of paid interns matriculated from these same schools.[19] Specifically, paid interns attended some of the top private universities that disproportionately enroll students from economically privileged backgrounds and where Black and Latino students are underrepresented. Although these data are just from the first year that Congress started to pay some of its interns, they fit within an existing pattern of how work opportunities remain the preserve of White and affluent communities within the congressional workplace.

And, while we often think of interns primarily as college students, this is not always the case. Internships are marketed as valuable experiences for college students and for their ability to be counted toward college credit (even though many universities charge students to count their internships toward their degree). But some interns arc also recent graduates who are plotting out their careers and trying to earn a living. There are others, long graduated from college and sometimes with advanced degrees, who also intern. As congressional employment becomes more competitive and remains just as insular, internships, many of which are unpaid, have become an unexpected way for those with a postsecondary degree to get a job on the Hill.

Deidre, for instance, was a Black attorney with an expertise in tax policy when she became an intern. She confided to me that she naively thought that when she moved to Washington, "I can just walk into Ways and Means, lay down my credentials, and I would get a job." Deidre quickly found out, after getting no hits on her applications, that it did not matter *what* she knew, what mattered more was *who* she knew. She applied to be an intern after her friends who lived in Washington told her how networking and Hill experience was important for getting a job. She landed an unpaid internship with her local congressman, working three to four days a week. She explained, "At the beginning of my internship, I was living on my savings and living with a friend, rent free. However, I eventually found a part-time job as a retail sales associate."

Once on the Hill, she used her insider status to network and meet other staffers. Eventually she found a mentor, a Black man with decades of experiences on the Hill. Compared to the difficulty she had as an outsider getting onto the Hill, she described the process of finding a job as a newly minted insider rather straightforward. "A position came open. I applied, with his help, of course, and went in on his recommendation. And I eventually ended up getting a job." Her mentor's recommendation carried significant weight in the Black lawmaker's office where she applied, as both offices frequently worked together.

Even though Deidre eventually found a job, the whole hiring process was off-putting and diminished her idealized view of the legislature. Candidly, she told me, "I happen to resent that this type of institution could not appreciate what I had to offer." It did not matter that she was highly credentialed, had expertise in tax policy and the highest grades in the tax policy courses she took in law school. It did not matter that she had political experience running a field office for Barack Obama during the 2008 presidential election. Even with these experiences it was hard to land an unpaid internship. She applied to work as an intern for numerous lawmakers who served on the Ways and Means Committee but was only able to find an internship for a lawmaker that represented the state where she lived. What's more, even after she landed her full-time staff position, she continued working part-time in the same retail job she had as an intern for three years.

Keisha and Deidre were not the only the Black staffers I interviewed who started their careers as congressional interns. Carla, a senior Senate staffer, started as a press intern for her home state senator. After she finished college, her chief of staff called and offered her a junior staff position. Melissa, another Black woman who had been the chief of staff for two representatives, first interned for her local congressman and then a senior Democratic leader in the House. Walter, a legislative director for a White Democrat representative, interned through the Congressional Black Caucus Foundation (CBCF), whose long-standing internship and fellowship program has created an important pipeline for Black staff representation. As he put it, "The CBCF internship provided an opportunity for someone like myself who did not come from a family of extraordinary means to be able to live in Washington, DC, and have some money to support myself while there."

The CBCF fellowship program operates similarly to the foundation's internship program, but it places Black professionals with advanced educational degrees into congressional offices. Kelly was pursuing her master's degree in the late 1990s when she became a CBCF fellow. After her fellowship she stayed in her office for two more years as a junior staffer and then returned years later to serve as chief of staff for several members. She described how the fellowship program provided her entry into Congress and, more importantly, ensured that money didn't get in the way. When I asked her if there were barriers to entering this world, she said:

> I do think there are and those were barriers I did not face because of the opportunity that the Black Caucus Foundation gave me. And it's primarily for me, in my view, it is economics. You know, a lot of people can come to town, they can afford even the cheapest, seediest apartment in town . . . but that still takes a lot of money in DC. And they can afford to delay independently living, I didn't have to do that. I could come here and others can come here,

knowing that they have families that will support them. You know, in the case of CBCF we have a stipend, my parents were supportive, and so they sent me money and gave me money, where I could go home on the weekends or whatever. And I think those are the types of barriers that really disproportionately affect Black students or Black young professionals because they can't afford to basically come here and work for free and not have some of their expenses supported by families, who may have just struggled to get them through college.

While it is easy to understand how unpaid internships and fellowships are out of reach for many Black men and women who come from poor and working-class families, these unpaid positions can even be out of reach for those who belong to the Black middle class.

Sociologists have long documented the precarity of the Black middle class and how distinct this group is from the White middle class.[20] The Black middle class lags behind the White middle class in nearly all of the key indicators of middle-class status, from income to wealth to housing. The median Black household has about half of the income of the median White household. Racial disparities in household wealth are even greater. The wealth of the median Black household stands at about $15,000 compared to $140,000 for the median White household. This difference in wealth is akin to owning a car versus owning a small home.[21]

Even families at the top of the Black middle class lag behind their White counterparts. Patrick Sharkey finds that "households in the elite Black middle class—that is, households making more than $100,000 per year—live in communities that have greater levels of disadvantage, and that are surrounded by communities with greater disadvantage, than even low-income White households making less than $30,000 per year."[22] These economic disparities have real costs for Black families. For example, racial wealth disparities lead Black students to take on more debt and riskier types of debt than White students to finance their education.[23] When we consider both the costs of education and the type of prestigious institutions that Black students need to attend to obtain high-paying jobs, we can see how race and class act as intersecting and overlapping forces that shape who works in Congress.

The career trajectories of all of these Black staffers underscore how congressional internships provide an important pathway into a notoriously insular institution. For Keisha, it gave her a working knowledge of how congressional offices operate and a keen understanding of which positions held the most influence. Furthermore, it initiated a years-long relationship with her lawmaker, which allowed her to bypass the traditional hiring process and come in with more seniority. As Deidre demonstrated, internships also allow young professionals to cultivate social relationships with staffers, who are gatekeepers for congressional employment. She was able to find a veteran staffer who could vouch for her during the hiring process. However, as her experience illustrates, taking an internship can be financially costly. In her case, it meant deferring compensation for the promise of future employment at the same time that her peers from law schools would probably be starting high-salaried jobs. These types of unequal work arrangements have long-term consequences for staffers' salaries and savings if the only way they can get a job in Congress means they must work for free. It also shapes the racial face of our democracy—Deidre and Keisha are exceptions that demonstrate the rule of Black exclusion.

The Power and Limits of Black Social Networks

Internships are important because they create and sustain relationships between Hill insiders and those who aspire to be them. As we have seen, for some, internships are essential for creating social relationships that would not otherwise exist. Other people, of course, already have preexisting relationships with Hill insiders and other Washington politicos. These instrumental social connections can exist between family, friends, classmates, or previous coworkers. Not surprisingly, the question of who has these preexisting relationships, and who doesn't, is answered at the intersection of inequalities, especially of race, class, and gender.

For decades, sociologists have studied the relationship between hiring, social networks, and race.[24] This research builds on a core sociological finding: people find jobs, and often the best jobs, through people they know rather than through an intermediary service or direct application.[25] And the returns of this social process are uneven for Black and White job seekers. White job seekers benefit more from social networks in employment because Black Americans are often excluded from the networks that are instrumental for hiring and promotions.[26] What's more, sociologists David Pedulla and Devah Pager found that Black job seekers must work twice as hard using their social contacts to get the same results as White job seekers.[27]

These network dynamics also unfold on the Hill. If you grew up in a poor and racially segregated community, or attended a less prestigious university, the chances of you being a part of social networks necessary to get onto Capitol Hill are slim. Among the Black staffers I spoke with only a few came from elite families. What that meant, and what I frequently heard passed along as advice to young Black professionals, was that they needed to network and build the social connections that they did not have. Since I interviewed Black staffers employed on the Hill, I saw again and again how networks worked, rather than how they failed. For those who found their job through social networks it could make the job search process feel effortless and serendipitous, and at other times it could feel exhausting because it meant constantly creating and nurturing relationships. Nevertheless, so many people I spoke with emphasized how lucky they were to get a job because even this pathway was uncertain. These social mechanisms of inclusion reveal the nature of Capitol Hill exclusion.

Kyle was the only Black staffer I spoke with who had a parent that previously worked in Congress. When he looked to transition from a career in commercial litigation to politics he sought the advice of his dad, who worked in the Senate in the 1980s. His dad put him in touch with staffers who worked for Senator Harry Reid, who at the time was the Senate minority leader. Kyle knew little about the congressional hiring process but through these personal introductions he learned about the social world upon which Capitol Hill is built. They told him about how jobs were posted and the process for application. Perhaps more importantly, they gave him entry into this insular space because "by the time they're posted they usually know who they want."

He applied to be a senior legislative assistant for a Democratic senator but because he lacked previous Hill experience, the office offered him a position as a legislative correspondent. His dad, also a lawyer, advised him against taking this entry-level position. He told him, "If you're a lawyer and you come in at this position you cannot move up." Kyle explained, "I was going to take a huge salary cut and I might have had to sit next to somebody who just recently graduated from college." He eventually landed a position as a legislative aide, a slightly more senior role

than the previous one, working for a White Democratic senator. He stayed in that position for approximately a year until
he left for a more senior position in the House. Here, too, his
dad's social network helped advance his career.

Kyle and his dad attended a reception, one that was charac-
teristic of the many postwork social events Washington professionals attend, which unbeknownst to him would lead to his
next job. At the event, his dad was socializing with a friend, a
Black woman who was a chief of staff for a Black representative in the House. She mentioned a vacancy in her office in the
exact policy areas that Kyle specialized in. Of course, Kyle's
dad immediately recommended him for the position. This led
to Kyle meeting the chief of staff himself at the reception, followed by a meeting with the congressman later. This chance
encounter culminated in a job offer for a more senior position in the House, where Kyle would handle the congressman's committee work. A few years later Kyle transitioned to
the committee entirely. The fact that Kyle is unique among the
people I interviewed isn't too surprising: the relatively small
number of Black staffers employed in Congress during previous generations means that there are relatively few young
Black professionals who have parents with Hill experience.

Less direct familial relationships could also prove helpful.
Karen, a Black attorney who worked for several Black representatives, grew up in Washington, where her parents, both
attorneys, held distinguished careers in the public and private
sectors. She was blunt about the fact that her family pedigree and
the exposure it brought mattered. "My first experience working on the Hill was as an unpaid intern in the summer working
for a member and it was just a summer job. The person who
was the chief of staff at the time was also a family friend and
she had asked me if I wanted to come check it out." After college, she decided to return to the Hill. "I reached out to staff in

an office I met through my dad and his work and I ended up getting a job in his office as his scheduler."

On the other hand, Cole, a Black man, got his first job through the help of his sister, who previously worked for a Republican senator. As he explained, "She had left the Hill already, but she had laid the groundwork." She introduced him to a well-known Hill staffer, a Black woman, who many affectionately referred to as the "Godmother of the Senate." Many Black staffers talked about her as a legendary figure who championed congressional staff diversity and helped get Black professionals jobs. I unsuccessfully tried multiple times to interview her about the more than thirty years' experience she had working on the Hill. Cole remembered his first meeting with the Godmother of the Senate:

> She literally just wanted to see me. She just asked me a few questions about, you know, who I was and where I was coming from. Just real general stuff. Not even like, hey, do you have your college degree? It wasn't even anything like that. It was just like she had my resume. We walked the stretch of the hallway and then she was like, all right, well, you're good. I'll let you know if I hear anything. And literally that was the entire conversation. Like five minutes. Maybe even less.

About a month later, Cole was contacted by a Senate office for an entry-level staff position. He went through the standard interview process, which included talking with several different staffers before he was hired. But he emphasized that his connection to the Godmother of the Senate was crucial. He was hired, in part, because someone owed her a favor for hiring someone else. After working in that office for a few months as a staff assistant, he transitioned to working for a Senate committee. The way he got this next job was in a similar insider fashion. As he remembered, he knocked on a door to a committee office to deliver a document, when he encountered an older woman that was retiring. He recalled her looking him over and saying he would be perfect for her job. She then forwarded his resume to a chief of staff, who called him back for an interview.

Cole's hiring stories demonstrate the absurdity of insider connections on the Hill. While not every inside connection unfolds like this, it is unnerving to know that it sometimes can. What's more, his repeated use of "literally" suggests that he was even in disbelief over how easy it could be to get a job if you knew someone on the inside. While this moment demonstrates that not only White men can benefit from nepotism, it also creates a depressing outlook for racial and class equity, if getting in sometimes means walking down the hallway or knocking on the door of the right person. Especially considering that when I interviewed Cole, he was among the few Black legislative directors in the House.

For some, knowing the right person was a member in their family, for others it was their friends. John was one of the highest-ranking Black staffers in the Senate during the 1990s. He was working as an attorney in Washington when a close college friend told him about an opportunity to work for a moderate Republican senator. The two had played basketball in college—rivals for their respective Ivy League universities—and stayed in touch as they lived and worked in Washington. After his friend notified John of the vacancy, he connected him with Vernon Jordan, a powerful Black civil rights leader who advised Democratic and Republican leaders. As he tells it, "Vernon had been doing a lot of work supporting the senator, because the senator was very strong in the civil rights community." Additionally, as the epigraph illustrates, Jordan had long been a critic of racial inequality on the Hill. John told me about his meeting with Vernon Jordan, which led to him getting hired by the senator:

> I'm sitting in the office of the venerable Vernon Jordan. And you look on his wall—and this kind of stuff mattered to me—you saw three big photos on his wall of his shaking hands with the last three presidents. And these weren't posed shots, these were walking on the White House grounds and "Hi, Mr. President, how are you?" kind of photos. And so, you know . . . those kinds of things are impactful.
>
> We're talking, he's interviewing me. And it turned out I knew his daughter from New York. I knew her through my sisters. We kibitzed about all that. Next thing I know he picks up the phone, and what appeared to be a direct line to the senator, called and said, "I got somebody better than you deserve." You know, they sort of bantered back and forth. "And I'm gonna have him up there this afternoon."
>
> So, I pull my scheduler out of my pocket, just sort of pretending that I've had some conflicts, knowing full well whatever was there I was getting that out of the way 'cause this is an opportunity to get up there, and that he was opening his door for me. And so later that afternoon I got up there. I may have sat with him, I don't know, maybe an hour? Hour and a half? And then got together with his chief of staff.

After meeting with the senator and his chief of staff, John joined the office as counsel and worked his way up to chief of staff a short time later. When John was promoted, there were no other Black chiefs of staff employed in the Senate, nor were there any Black senators when he started out. His history-making employment hinged on knowing the right people.

These career histories present two important takeaways about the organization of the congressional workplace and Black social networks. First, in their own words, Black staffers' accounts underscore how, for the day-to-day business of American lawmaking, politics is relational, and social relationships are foundational. These same qualities are just as true for Black people, even though we predominately think of this system as designed to benefit White people. Second, Cole's and John's career histories show the power of Black social networks. They demonstrate how Black professionals get onto the Hill through a small group of highly influential Black men and women who have the attention of lawmakers and senior staffers. At the same time, these examples demonstrate the narrow pathways for Black employment in Congress. These powerful Black figures are not widely accessible. The Black staffers I interviewed were connected to them through family and friends.

While some Black men and women already had preexisting social networks they could rely on for information and recommendations, others had to work to expand who they knew. Shanise just finished law school when she decided to pursue a career on the Hill. She used a snowball technique to build her social network based upon people she knew from a previous Senate internship and political campaign. "After the campaign was over, anyone who I had a good connection with—I said, 'Look. I'm trying to make my way to DC, I wanna work on the Hill. Do you know anybody who lives in DC—anyone that I could meet with that would be helpful?" At the time she lived in North Carolina, so she traveled hundreds of miles to DC to pound the pavement and get her name out there.

She remembered doing this week-long sojourn at least twice before she got a hit. "So, one day I get a phone call from a young lady who was like a mentor to me. I met her through a campaign. And she's like, 'Hey—chief of staff has a job for you—he wants you to call him, here's his number.'" Initially, Shanise was confused because her mentor was not the person who introduced her to the chief of staff, it was another gentleman she worked with on a campaign. Unbeknownst to Shanise, these two contacts had previously worked together and recommended her for the open position.

> Apparently my name had come up in discussions, and they both were trying to introduce me to the same person, and so once that guy had two people vouching for me, he went, "Oh, she must be someone. Because now that two different people who know her gave me her resume."

Political campaigns are a natural stepping stone to Capitol Hill. However, campaigns that rely heavily on unpaid labor are unsurprisingly not racially diverse.[28] On the other hand, Black social groups, on and off the Hill, are very effective at cultivating these necessary social connections. On the Hill, Black staff groups work to demystify the *legislative black box*. Sociologist Shanelle Haile finds that Black staff groups act as brokers that compensate for the lack of institutional support and opaqueness in congressional hiring.[29] The most popular are the Senate Black Legislative Staff Caucus and Congressional Black Associates. I attended numerous forums where organizers, who occupied mid- and senior-level positions, provided guidance and advice for hiring and promotions. Junior staffers made up most attendees, and a few Black professionals from across the city would attend these meetings to learn how they could become a part of this exclusive group.

In one event sponsored by the Congressional Black Associates, for example, organizers assembled five of the highest-ranking Black staffers in the House. Among the panelists were two chiefs of staff, one staff director, a floor director, and a senior aide to the Speaker. The panelists recounted their career journeys to a packed audience in an ornate room in the Cannon office building. They spoke about hard work, persistence, and doing their best to distinguish themselves from their peers as key to getting to the top. However, the ability to be in the room and meet Hill insiders mattered more than any general advice that they offered. At the end of these meetings, attendees would head directly to the presenters to get their business cards and establish a more formal connection. This is also how I would meet other Hill staffers myself. In one meeting for Black men on the Hill, Congressman Hakeem Jeffries spoke about his political career. After he finished, the organizer led a round of introductions for the fifty attendees, mostly Black male staffers, to get to know one another in the crowded narrow room in the basement of the Capitol. Among them was a Black woman who sat in the back. Her introduction included a pitch about her seven years of public relations experience that she was hoping to leverage to become a deputy communications director. She explained she was joining every organization possible in hope of making a connection to obtain a Hill position.

Black sororities and fraternities are another important social group. For example, Tracy never thought about a career in Congress until her Delta Sigma Theta sorority sister, who she visited in DC, encouraged her to think about working on the Hill and circulated her resume. "It was actually a sorority sister of mine who had been on the Hill for almost twenty years that got my resume and gave it to people." Her resume found its way to the office of a White Democratic representative, who called her for an interview and then hired her as a staff assistant. The whole process was serendipitous. "I got the call for the interview just before graduation, like, the day before graduation. So, it was very quick, and I didn't even have a chance to think about it." Without this type of social relationship, which provided insider access, it would be difficult for someone like Tracy to get a job in Congress. She grew up poor and experienced living in shelters and sleeping in cars. She noted that this hardship set her apart from staffers on the Hill, White and Black alike, who had more privileged backgrounds. Despite this hardship, she excelled in school and earned scholarships to attend a prominent Historically Black College. In college, she found herself focusing on finishing school. "I was in a place where I really wanted to just be done with school. I wanted to get over that hurdle and it was hard to kind of think about next steps because for an undergraduate who comes from poverty, you never really escape it."

In her life, Tracy experienced the proximate effects of extreme poverty, including homelessness, and dealt with its far-reaching consequences, including the inability to engage in future planning. However, someone from a disadvantaged background like hers is not likely to end up on Capitol Hill. Congressional employment requires prospective staffers to plot out their futures in advance and to absorb the high costs to entry—namely unpaid internships—along the way. Coupled together, inequality and exclusivity undermine representation in Congress, both in terms of who works there and how issues are understood. Tracy brought firsthand knowledge about what it means to be poor to her job as a legislative assistant covering poverty and hungry issues. However, her presence was by chance: she happened to meet the right people on a visit to Washington right as she began to think about her career.

In all, Black social networks are important because they help Black professionals get their foot in the door. At the same time, these networks are limited because there is no telling when the door will open. As sociologist Alejandro Portes notes, transactions involving social capital are associated with uncertain time horizons because there is no telling how and when these relationships will matter.[30] In this way, while Black social networks help overcome exclusionary barriers related to nontransparency, we cannot expect them to be an institutional solution to unequal hiring processes.

Narrow Pathways

Everyone had their own story about how they got on the Hill. They enthusiastically retold their career journeys like an adventure tale, filled with twists and turns that ultimately ended with them securing the grand prize, a job in the second most powerful workplace in Washington. Although the people in these stories were different, their paths were not. Staffers got onto the Hill through three main routes: social relationships, internships, and direct application.

The paths Black staffers take is not fundamentally different from the strategies that White staffers use, but it is narrower. Their experiences allow me to tell two stories at once—how existing congressional hiring practices promote inequality overall, and the specific ways that Black staffers are impacted. I found that for Black staffers, to use these same strategies they had to be plugged into elite Black networks and have impeccable credentials. Membership in these groups often comes with steep costs in the forms of unpaid labor. The Black staffers that I interviewed had to be anything but ordinary to make it onto the Hill.

While I interviewed many Black staffers who had successfully obtained internships and used these experiences to land full-time jobs, their presence—and relative success—doesn't change the underlying reality that people of color are underrepresented as congressional interns. Unequal access and inadequate compensation for this entry-level position lay the groundwork for a racially and economically stratified legislature that enhances the power of White staffers to participate in areas of policymaking, oversight, and representation;

it similarly limits the influence of staffers of color to do the same.[31] Moreover, this inequality also shapes the cultivation of our political leaders.

On Capitol Hill, it is often said that today's interns are tomorrow's members of Congress. One prominent example of this pathway is former Speaker of the House Nancy Pelosi, who interned for Maryland Senator Daniel Brewster along with former House Majority Leader Steny Hoyer.[32] Unfortunately, most congressional interns are White. Similar to the underrepresentation of racial minorities in the congressional workplace at large, this problem persists because of a lack of transparency. The opaqueness in the administration of congressional internships fuels inequality on Capitol Hill and affects the racial makeup of future staffers and lawmakers.

Besides interning, another strategy to getting hired on the Hill was social connections. Almost everyone I encountered told me about the value of networking: newcomers and old-timers; Republicans and Democrats; Black and White staffers alike. This advice was often repeated in mentoring events for Black staffers that I attended. This advice is well intentioned but misses the mark. Telling Black applicants and other applicants of color to network for career advancement obscures the main problem: the supremacy of White social networks. White staffers dominate congressional staff positions, and the reliance on insular hiring methods allows them to hoard job opportunities and political power for themselves. Black social networks simply cannot compete against White social networks, which are more numerous, widespread, and consequently more influential. At best, Black social networks can maintain Black staff representation and assist in growing this population incrementally. At worst, it limits job opportunities to a well-educated and well-connected Black elite. The Black staffers I interviewed were a part of this Black elite. Some had

parents who held top jobs in government and other leading private industries. Others were first-generation students
at selective universities and had obtained advanced degrees.
Either through family or education they obtained social connections that could help them get onto the Hill. Although many
Black professionals successfully found congressional staff positions through their social networks, the specificity of this path
to success ensures that it is not a widely accessible pathway.

Exclusive barriers to the congressional workplace threaten
our endeavor toward a multiracial democracy and antiracist
future. Deidre, the attorney who could only get hired on the
Hill by first taking an unpaid internship, explained to me that
making it inside Congress was important because she felt it
was a space where racism could be dismantled. She told me that,
on some days, when she is walking in the Capitol, she pauses to
take it all in. She says to herself, "Wow. This is where I am, this
is where it all happens." She referred to Congress as the place
where slavery and de jure segregation was abolished. Now that
she was in the Capitol, she saw her role as advancing lawmaking to achieve racial justice. "I also have a responsibility now
that I'm here. I wasn't there then. But I'm here now. What can
I do to help to move us forward on some issues that are really
plaguing our communities?"

CHAPTER THREE

The Nod

MAKING BLACKNESS VISIBLE

*I am a man of substance, of flesh and bone, fiber and liquids—
and I might even be said to possess a mind. I am invisible,
understand, simply because people refuse to see me.*

—RALPH ELLISON[1]

*To my fellow Non-American Blacks:
In America, You Are Black, Baby Dear Non-American Black.
When you make the choice to come to America, you become
Black. Stop arguing. Stop saying I'm Jamaican or I'm
Ghanaian. America doesn't care. You must nod back when a
Black person nods at you in a heavily White area. It is called
the Black nod. It is a way for Black people to say, "You are not
alone, I am here too."*

—CHIMAMANDA ADICHIE[2]

BLACK MEN AND women nod to one another wherever we are,
whether it is on 125th Street in Harlem, or traveling abroad,
or—as one Black chief of staff told me—in line for a ride at

Disney World.[3] Explaining the significance of the nod for Black men, Michael Eric Dyson writes: "The point, after all, is to unify Black men across barriers of cash, color, or culture into a signifying solidarity."[4] Exchanged among Black men of different social status, the nod, he contends, is visual Ebonics, expressing Black cool and a subtle recognition of each other. But the Black nod is not just for men. In *Americanah*, Ifemelu, the Nigerian female protagonist, explains to other Black immigrants the specific cultural rules they must abide by in the United States. The Black nod is taught to Black newcomers and also younger generations. For example, when Andre Johnson, the main character on the hit ABC sitcom *Black-ish*, discovered his eldest son, Andre Jr., was not nodding to other Black students in his majority-White school, it became the premise of an entire episode.[5] To this end, the nod is particularly salient in spaces where Black presence is minimal or nonexistent, like Congress. In these circumstances, the nod takes on an additional meaning—it transforms from a common cultural gesture to an important act of witnessing. It is a recognition between Black participants—a recognition of themselves, the social setting, and the role of race.[6]

We have seen how hard it is to access an insular institution like Congress, especially for Black men and women. But now that they have made it inside, what is it like for them day to day? Here we will focus on what it feels like to work in a White space. And we will do that by analyzing one tiny, but vital, part of that daily life. I believe that the Black nod encapsulates, in a seemingly banal motion, the contours of Black life on the Hill. The Black nod, in other words, is a synecdoche for the racial landscape of Congress.

During the summers of 2010–13, I worked as a legislative intern in my old office in the House as I collected data for this book. As part of my duties, I was often called upon to run errands for senior staffers in the office. Several times a day, I would be asked to go from our office in the Rayburn building through the tunnels to the House Floor to drop off legislation, or to the offices of the other members to get them to sign bills, or to twenty other places around the Hill. These tasks were mundane and never glamorous. But it was a great way to collect data. I recorded my interactions with Black workers, whether it was a nod, smile, or conversation. I never initiated the nod or communicated while walking in the hallways unless I knew the employees, so that I would minimize my own influence on interactions I observed. I then followed up on these observations in my interviews with Black staffers.

I asked Black staffers about their relationships with their peers, and specifically with other Black workers. During these moments, they, either independently or with prompting, would discuss intra-racial interactions, including the nod. I would have them teach me about the nod, its meaning, how the gesture unfolded, and explain why they participated. These discussions naturally expanded to cover what it meant to be Black and working in Congress. They discussed their perceptions of how race unfolded in their daily work life and careers. Probing about habitual gestures allowed Black staffers, somewhat unknowingly, to articulate how the institutional and historical context in which they are embedded shaped their daily experiences. In a few cases, at the end our conversations, staffers would tell me, quite comically, I should study the Black nod!

Safety and Strength in Numbers

Kelly, the top staffer for a Republican representative who earlier told us about how a paid internship initiated her political career, explained the meaning of the Black nod on the Hill in this way. "If it's an African American staffer, I mean,

I still think that same old-fashioned kind of nod is still done up here. You don't really think about it, you just kind of do it. And it's a very subtle, 'I see you.'" She explained, "I do think that it's just a recognition on the part of all of us that there are so few, and it's still, even though it shouldn't be new or fresh, it kinda sorta is, because there is still such a long way to go. So, it's just sort of an acknowledgement. Good job, you made it." As you might remember Kelly started out on the Hill in the 1990s as a legislative fellow. More than a decade later, her own circumstances had changed, a lot, but the status and number of Black staffers, overall, had not.

As we have seen, the congressional workplace is really, really White. Black staffers repeatedly explained that the nod was motivated, in large part, by their numerical underrepresentation in the congressional workplace. Of the forty-two Black staffers I interviewed, thirty-seven (88 percent) knew about the nod, and thirty-four (80 percent) participated in the practice. Additionally, twenty-nine respondents (60 percent) said—either directly or indirectly—that the nod was a gesture of solidarity and referred to their numerical underrepresentation. What this meant was that Black staffers felt compelled to acknowledge other Black men and women when they saw them in the hallways; it did not matter if they were of the opposing party. Political distinctions did not matter because they all shared a common racial experience. Being a Black staffer meant experiencing a whole range of feelings inseparable from race: frustration, loneliness, disrespect, and stress. This shared racial experience meant that Black staffers needed to stick together.

Sean, a junior staffer for a White Democratic representative, was among the Black staffers I spoke with who emphatically stated that they always greeted other Black workers in the Capitol. "The nod is just a way of communicating, not orally, of acknowledging their presence. For me personally, I'm just acknowledging, 'Oh, you're me, but you're you. You're Black.' I make a point to acknowledge every single Black person I see." Randall, a senior Democratic committee staffer, told me, "It is acknowledging a shared experience we have. I even try to talk to Black Republicans because I know they have it tough." He alludes to how there are fewer African Americans in Republican offices and the Republican Party in general.[7] He perceives that their situation must be exhausting and communicates his support through friendly gestures, like the nod.

Anthony, a Republican committee staffer, told me, "I could not live with myself if I didn't nod." To him nodding meant, "I'm in the struggle, 'I see you brother, I see you sister.' I see the struggle." Despite what others might think, he confided to me that he did not feel any racial hostility in his office, but he did not believe the same could be said about White Democratic offices. "Black staffers go through a lot, those not in CBC [Congressional Black Caucus] offices, hearing racist comments or comments that make you pause to say, 'Why do you say something like that or talk about a group in a certain way?'" Similarly, a Black legislative assistant explained his participation this way: "Well, I nod to a lot of Blacks in the hallway because I know them. But I try to go out of my way to nod to them because you never know what they are going through. Someone might be having a tough day, especially if they are working in a non-CBC office, you just never know."

Cassie, who did work for a Black lawmaker as a legislative fellow, explained her participation in the Black nod this way:

> Again, I think it is the sense of relief in the day-to-day stress, the craziness of the Hill. Because you always feel like you are fighting, you know, you always feel like you are trying to prove something and do something. And you can sometimes feel overwhelmed, and you know you

are not always necessarily supported but to know in that brief moment that someone else is acknowledging you and going through the same thing you are going through. It is just a respite, you know.

All staffers work long and unpredictable hours, and often for low salaries. What's more, they are not given much support and training to do their job—which makes their days even more stressful.[8] However, staffers of color have the additional burden of racism, which can manifest as overt discrimination and as the pressures associated with being the only member of your racial group in the room. The nod is simply a way to recognize this shared reality, a way for Black staffers to express their camaraderie and support when they see each other.

Jonathan, a chief of staff for a White representative, vehemently practiced the Black nod and told me how nodding was pervasive throughout the Hill when he started his career there over two decades prior. He fondly remembered, "When I started here in '91, that head nod was in full effect." He recalled meeting Black members of Congress like Kweisi Mfume, Ron Dellums, and Barbara Collins through informal greetings and gestures in the hallways. He explained to me how he introduced himself to Black lawmakers when he was a young staffer:

> Yeah, either a nod or—you could also say, "Good morning, congressman," they're like, "Oh, hey, good morning, how are you?" . . . You could see—John Lewis, you could say hello. They would say hi. You see Lewis does that all the time, 'cause everybody now *sees* him. He—Lewis—could walk by everybody and just be like, "I don't wanna talk to you. You know who I am?"

Here, Jonathan references a critical dimension of the Black nod: its ability to transcend occupational rank. Even Black members of Congress nod. And just as importantly, menial staffers use the nod with those powerful members of Congress. Jonathan also details how he and other African Americans who have accrued a certain level of success could easily abandon these social practices, but instead they remain committed to them. "I could come into my office every day, sit at my desk, and pat myself on the back for eight hours at what I've achieved and where I am. I don't have to say a doggone thing to anybody. Because most of 'em can't do anything for me. But the ironic thing is I go out of my way to make contact with people." Jonathan went on to explain the value of nodding and having core networks of African Americans for the purposes of venting about certain issues to which they would be able to relate to and seek their professional mentorship. Sociologist Michèle Lamont found that Black working-class men strongly valued solidarity and generosity, and here, these principles are found among Black professional men.[9]

Building Community One Nod at a Time

But the nod is not merely a means of showing support. The gesture does far more: it helps cultivate and nurture social relationships, which is key for professional advancement. In one particular meeting for Black men on the Hill, I was part of a group that was explicitly told to nod. The informal meet-up was for all Black men on the Hill: members, House and Senate staffers, and service employees. Although the focus of this meeting was on Black men's health and policy initiatives to address racial health disparities, one of the organizers prefaced the formal proceedings by explaining the purpose of the group. A primary concern of the leaders of the group was to build stronger social ties among Black men on the Hill to facilitate professional advancement. The organizer stressed the importance of networks and building stronger social ties with other Black men so they could be privy to information outside their personal network. Consequently, the staffer instructed those in attendance to nod and acknowledge "brothas" when they met in the hallways. The nod, in other words, is not only a recognition of camaraderie; it is a means of connection. The nod, although just a brief greeting, could also be a moment that leads to the formation of more substantive relationships.

While most of the nods I recorded from Black staffers were fleeting moments accompanied with brief salutations, the nod did on occasion set the stage for interacting more substantively with Black staffers. In one instance, a young Black staffer nodded to me while I waited for the elevator on the third floor of Rayburn. He lamented, "This elevator is so slow," before asking, "What office do you work for?" He then told me about how he had worked on and off for a senior Black representative for the last seven years. As we descended several floors on the elevator, I formally introduced myself to him. As we departed, he said, "I will see you around." And, in fact, we did continue to see each other around, on the Hill and in Washington. After I concluded my fieldwork, I ran into him at a mutual friend's graduation party on the Georgetown Waterfront. I still run into him to this day, and I always laugh to myself because it is written in my notes how our friendship began with a nod.

Another stand-out moment during my fieldwork was when I attended a packed forum sponsored by the Washington Government Relations Group, an association of Black lobbyists and consultants, to increase Black representation on the Hill and K Street. I listened for over an hour as six Black professionals discussed their careers and provided advice to young Black and Brown staffers and interns. After the panel concluded, I introduced myself to the panelists. I then had to find my way out through the throngs of young staffers, who were also trying to get the panelists' business cards and set up meetings to follow up on their advice. As I finally approached the door of the cramped meeting room, an older Black man sitting on the edge of a small table asked me what I learned. He introduced himself as Ray, a former Hill staffer and current lobbyist, and then asked me what office I worked in. I explained that I was not a Hill staffer but rather I was studying them. In the moments that passed, Ray acted as an avuncular figure, quizzing me about my research and the event. He then connected me to current and former Black staffers in the room. "Do you know Audrey? You should speak to Audrey, everyone knows Audrey. Audrey come here, meet James. He is doing a study on Black staffers!" I was elated as the interaction unfolded and I became acquainted with Audrey and so many other Black staffers. The moment was remarkable for me as a researcher but typical for Ray. He saw it as his duty to acknowledge Black professionals and connect them to one another.

Ray started in Washington as a staffer for a freshman representative in the 1990s. Even though he watched C-SPAN since its first broadcast, he never considered a career as a congressional staffer or lobbyist because he never knew these occupations existed. He got into politics by chance after he graduated from law school and was looking for a job. A friend arranged an interview for him with a young African American running for Congress. After the election, he took a position as a legislative correspondent and then quickly received a promotion to legislative assistant a few weeks later. As Ray explained, this was an exciting period to work in Congress. At the time, the CBC was the largest it had ever been, and the possibility of affecting real change was immense. What's more, he understood the individual importance as a Black man working in Congress. "I was very clear, you know, when I walked those hallways and I look at that building and I know slaves helped to build that thing or did in fact build it—or cast the statue up there, I was aware of that. And I definitely had a sense of, look at me, I'm the surviving guy of all of that."[10]

One moment did stand out from his congressional career about what it meant to be a Black man working in a historically White space. He remembered walking in the Cannon House Office Building and noticing a young African American man coming toward him with a bunch of papers in hand. "I'm witnessing him walking in and out of different offices dropping off this piece of paper." Originally, he thought the gentleman might be a mailman. He continued his close observations, even noticing the sweat coming from his body. When they finally approached one another, he told me, "We nodded and started a conversation." He learned that the young man was not delivering mail, but rather resumes. Ray then explained how the congressional job market operated, saying, "No, that's not how you do that here."

As we have come to know, to get a job on the Hill you need an inside connection. Ray instantly became that person for this aspiring staffer. He directed the young Black man back to his office and introduced him to his chief of staff. After the introduction, his boss offered him an internship while he looked for a full-time staff job. Ray explained that, from there, his acquaintance turned coworker landed a position as a staff assistant for a White representative. After that stint, he transitioned to working for a Black representative, where he ultimately became a district director. This is a top staff position, which oversees the management and operation of congressional field offices. Reflecting on the friendship that started with a nod, he said, "I'd like to think that was a person whose life I've influenced directly because I took him that day and said, 'No, don't pass out resumes like that. You will not get a job like that. Let me introduce you to someone,' and that introduction led to a twenty-year career he's had as a result of that. And he's not the only one."

The Black nod is part of Black professionals' cultural tool-kit, and they use the gesture to facilitate introductions and maintain social networks with other African Americans.[11] Whether it is Congress or another work setting, we know that who you know matters. The nod helps introduce strangers to one another, strengthen bonds between acquaintances, and reaffirm commitments among friends. Sometimes it only takes one small interaction to turn into a friendship, and other times it takes repeated contact. For many of the Black staffers I spoke with, it was difficult to recollect how relationships began, especially with regard to a habitual gesture that they rarely contemplated in any deep manner. However, when Black staffers discussed the importance of nodding and social networks, they described in a generalized way how the nod acted as a preamble to conversations where they could obtain important information or introduce themselves to new acquaintances. As such, it makes sense to think of the nod as a part of an available repertoire from which Black professionals draw upon to interact with known and unknown members of their racial group.

Invisibility and Disrespect

In all of the exchanges of the Black nod recorded in my field notes, eye contact is the crucial first step that determines if the nod will occur.[12] The signals that we convey with our eyes inform us if the other individual is open to communication. If eye contact is reciprocated and sustained, what follows is some type of facial expression, which is then elaborated by a verbal or nonverbal message. Renowned sociologist Erving Goffman calls this exchange *civil inattention*.[13] However, seeing the person and making eye contact takes on a deeper, symbolic meaning for Black staffers.

What made the nod meaningful for Black staffers was that it meant that other Black men and women saw them. It was an acknowledgment of their presence and a show of respect. This was significant because in encounters with Whites on the Hill they did not always receive this same recognition. When Whites did not establish eye contact with Black staffers, either intentionally or unintentionally, Black staffers perceived this as further evidence of their social invisibility in the legislature.

Monica, a chief of staff for a Black representative, was adamant about always acknowledging Black workers. When discussing other racial interactions, she explained to me:

> White men act like they don't *see* you in the hallway, they look straight ahead or near the floor. Especially White members [of Congress]. Some of them won't even look at you. They look every other way but at you. Sometimes I am in the elevator, and they just ignore me. I will say hi if I am in close quarters with someone, but they do not *see* you. They just say "Floor number three please," like I work here [in the elevator].

Her reflections bring to mind a not-too-distant time in our country's racial history when Whites avoided eye contact with Blacks to signal their subordinate status. When Whites refused to look at Blacks, whether as pedestrians on the street or domestics employed in their homes, it signaled their invisibility.[14] Similarly, in Congress, Black staffers like Monica found these moments significant because they symbolized White entitlement and disrespect.

You might be thinking, if a White person does not reciprocate eye contact in a congressional hallway that is not sufficient evidence of racism. Perhaps they just did not see them! Furthermore, Congress is a national workplace with staffers from all fifty states who bring with them the cultural dispositions of their local communities. Northeasterners notoriously avoid interactions with strangers (and some known acquaintances) in public, whereas Southerners and Midwesterners are more likely to acknowledge and engage in civil inattention and small pleasantries.

While it might be tempting to dismiss Black staffers' claims of racism, it would be largely unfounded to dismiss multiple people's accounts of the same phenomenon, interpreted the same way. The same act seen as innocuous by someone who is not a member of a given racial minority can be understood systematically differently by those who are members of that minority—which gives rise to copious literature and public discourse around microaggressions and racisms as perceived by that group.[15] Sociologists Joe Feagin and Melvin Sikes reveal that when Black Americans speak about racism, they do so reflecting upon their lived experiences as racial subjects, as well as their loved ones' experiences, and with an informed understanding of the country's dubious racist history.[16] Therefore, when Black staffers assess what happens in these singular moments with Whites, they do so weighing it against a trove of different data points in their individual and collective memory. This is not to completely discount other explanations, but this is to say, Black folks know racism when they see it.

Although Monica did not believe she was owed more deference as a chief of staff, perhaps she is. Chiefs of staff hold immense power on the Hill, second only to lawmakers. They oversee multiple offices; set protocols; and manage staff. In addition, they serve as political surrogates for their bosses, often standing in for them in meetings and representing them at events back home. Top staffers, like Monica, regularly interact with members. They have the same access to restricted locations in the Capitol and are a part of the confidential discussions in these rooms. In this way, chiefs of staff are given a lot of power and respect; however, despite her senior position and more than a decade on the Hill, she did not feel she had the respect of Whites. At the end of the interview, Monica added, "Don't think racism is dead on the Hill. Racism is alive and well. Some of it is obvious and some of it's covert." For her, the disrespect that she encountered was a part of how racism operated subtly on the Hill.

Lisa, a Black committee staffer, said about the nod, "It's a way for us to acknowledge each other in this environment where we're not really respected and not really affirmed." She explained, "We're not in a majority, chiefly—numerically. We're not making the main decisions. Black folks aren't in positions of power, controlling the budgets or making the major policy decisions. In order to accept this, it's a way to sort of acknowledge people in this kind of personal situation." To Lisa, it was not only that Blacks were not in positions of power, but it was about how they were treated day to day that mattered. She recalled this one moment interacting with White staffers:

> One year I was taking the elevator. I was trying to exit the elevator. Before I could get out, a young bunch of staffers rushed on in. It was mildly irritating. I said, "Excuse me." And the young woman comes, and says, "Excuse me," to me. And I thought, "Oh how rude."

Echoing Monica, Lisa pointed to White disrespect in the elevator; however, she blamed younger White staff.[17] She labeled them as, "entitled," "privileged," and "oblivious to all the world." In contrast, she observed that "a lot of the folks of color who seek to make eye contact, a lot of them happen to be Black." She did not think that Black staff are "perfect," but she believed they had a different upbringing, which valued acknowledging individuals.

As a chief of staff, Jordan had an unpredictable and busy schedule. Finding time to talk with him was a challenge. I spent an hour following him around Capitol Hill as he completed some errands on a Friday afternoon, which included a stop at a nearby bank, where he ran into his boss at the teller. He interpreted his participation in the Black nod with other Black congressional workers as meaning, "I know who you are and I see you. I see you and I validate you." Within the few seconds in which he might see another Black worker and nod, he explained how the ephemeral gesture expressed their linked fate:

> We may know nothing about each other, but we're here on the Hill, which is where—we know we're a small number there, and we're walking these halls knowing that we're doing something good, something connected to the same kind of work, and so, there's a recognition there. You know, whether it's a Black male or female, you got my nod. I hear you, I see you, you know, and that's the start of it. If there's nothing else, you got that.

The nod was just one way he recognized and participated within the Black community on the Hill. He also made a special effort to recognize Black blue-collar workers on the Hill, who he saw as fictive kin.[18] There were the Black women who worked in the cafeteria, one he affectionately referred to as sister and another he more properly acknowledged as Ms. Thelma, noting that she was in her seventies. There was also a young Black man who worked in the superintendent's office, who told Jordan almost daily that he resembled his uncle. In fact, the young man wanted to take a picture of Jordan to show his real-life uncle. This made Jordan think, "You know what? If this guy thinks I look so much like his uncle—I said,

'You're my nephew.' So I'm gonna call you nephew from now on." This type of recognition, specifically among Black laborers, was important to Jordan. As he explained, "They support us along the way and they keep us going." This was a sentiment that I frequently heard from Black Hill professionals about Black service workers on the Hill, whose physical contributions to lawmaking are rarely acknowledged. Despite his feelings of invisibility, Jordan felt this was a prideful moment to be Black and working in the Capitol. He witnessed firsthand how Black workers in various positions across the Capitol made a difference, in small and not small ways, in legislation, and in administrative and physical support, which collectively assisted lawmaking.

Like others, Jordan's participation in the nod is tied to the underrepresentation of Black staffers on the Hill. However, to him it was important to nod, not because Whites on the Hill did not acknowledge him, but rather because people off the Hill, outsiders, did not acknowledge the presence and contributions of Black staffers in lawmaking overall. He said:

> As an African American male, I don't know that anybody knows that we walk this place and that we have such an impact on what we do. And so, sometimes it's like Ralph Ellison's book, *Invisible Man*, you know? You are here when nobody knows you're here.

Monica, Lisa, and Jordan all discussed in different ways the invisibility of congressional Black employees, and, as senior staffers, all three talked about a level of recognition they should be afforded but did not receive. Monica and Lisa both felt ignored by White lawmakers and White staffers in the hallways and elevators. Monica thought the lack of interaction indicated how Whites were consciously ignoring her presence, or that it was an attempt to reduce her social status, while

Lisa saw the behavior of young Whites as disrespectful and ignorant of a Black minority. Jordan also articulated claims of social invisibility; his concerns were more about those outside of Capitol Hill who do not realize that African Americans occupy senior and influential roles in the legislature. While each grievance differs slightly, each articulates a need to affirm the presence of African Americans in Congress in social interaction, and the Black nod is one tool they use to recognize their African American colleagues.

There is little awareness by some Whites about this social practice—only one non-Black staffer knew about the nod, which in many ways confirms Black staffers' claim of invisibility if White staffers are ignorant of visible gestures. The gesture is subtle and discreet, and if the perceptions of Black respondents are true, then Whites who intentionally avoid establishing eye contact may not see the gesture at all, thus confirming their invisibility in Congress. However, the ephemeral gesture is successful in ways that more formal methods of recognition are not. Monica, who before said that White men did not notice her in the hallways, later expressed anxiety suggesting that Blacks in large numbers heighten the awareness of Whites to the presence of Blacks:

> I have to tell you what happened last week. I was downstairs with one of my girlfriends in the cafeteria and we ran into some other Black people we know. And I said, you know, we have to break it up before they start thinking we are plotting. But that never happens. You never see that many Black people together.

What Monica told me was expressed with a certain degree of levity to convey how rare it is for her to see many African Americans outside of her office due the vastness (and Whiteness) of the Capitol complex. However, there is also a hint of racial paranoia in her reflection, which is connected to how African Americans formally and informally interact.[19] The nod works in part because the subtle gesture is discreet and often unnoticeable by those who are not Black. In addition, without a cultural awareness of the meaning of the gesture, the coded message of racial solidarity and recognition becomes indecipherable to outsiders. Many Black employees may try to avoid very public interactions with other Black employees in part because of what it might signal to White employees. As Elijah Anderson observed among Black corporate executives, highly visible moments of congregating or fraternizing closely with other Blacks are boundary-heightening events.[20] Put simply, when African Americans gather it reminds Whites about the racial identity of their Black coworkers in a manner that exaggerates differences between them. This could work to the disadvantage of African Americans who at other times attempt to blur distinctions between themselves and their White colleagues, what Karyn Lacy refers to as inclusionary boundary work.[21]

When the Black Person Doesn't Nod Back

If nodding does various kinds of work—acknowledging a shared experience, building networks, signaling visibility— then what happens when you *don't* nod? It is not surprising that many Black staffers were frustrated when White staffers failed to acknowledge them, in one way or another. But Black staffers took even greater offense when other Blacks failed to do the same. Not nodding effectively allowed Black staffers to question non-nodders' racial authenticity and understanding of racial issues. Their criticism underscored the significance of race in their daily work experiences and careers. It is also a reflection of how race, and specifically Blackness, is performed.

I should note that there are obvious gender differences in the practice of nodding among African Americans. One female respondent said that Black women were more inclined to speak and that the nod was actually more of a male gesture.[22] However, another explanation is simply that nodding to Black men could be seen as a possible sexual signal, a layer of implication that Black men never worried about. Black women are careful that the gestures they exchange convey camaraderie, not sexual attraction. Therefore, female staffers said they were more likely to reciprocate the nod than initiate the gesture themselves. Nods, therefore, were typically between Black men, or from Black men to Black women. However, Black women were very aware of the Black nod and its significance and spoke at great length about the gesture.

"For me, it would be like, what kind of Black person are you?" Cassie, the legislative fellow, said with laughter. She continued, "Honestly, like how do I put that in a better way? Um, like, are you trying to ignore the fact that you are a Black person and I'm a Black person? Do you think race really doesn't matter?"

As Cassie said, it is more than just being blind to the continuing significance of race; there was a clear difference between the people who nod and those who do not. It is unclear from my interviews why some Black employees do not nod, as almost everyone I interviewed said they participated in the nod or another similar gesture. In interviews, Black staff presented themselves as friendly and social beings who acknowledge all Blacks and individuals who they came into close contact with. I was unable to find any Black staffer who was aware of the Black nod but told me they chose not to participate in any of these social practices.

Black employees who did not know the motivations of non-nodders inferred their own explanations. They routinely brought up class differences to explain the behavior of non-nodders, saying those who did not nod thought they were somehow better than the rest and were not enmeshed in the struggle for racial equality. If the nod meant "I see you," then not nodding meant, "I do not see you," which respondents described as uniquely hurtful coming from another African American.

In *Disintegration*, political journalist Eugene Robinson ruminates about the splintering of the Black community:[23]

> I have to ask whether Black Americans, divided as they are by the process of disintegration, still have enough shared experiences, values, hopes, fears, and dreams that they define and claim a single racial identity—and feel a racial solidarity powerful enough to connect, if only for an instant, strangers who may never see each other again. I give the little nod without even thinking about it. Is it my imagination, or are fewer people nodding back?

Similarly, former congressional Black employees of the 1980s and 1990s and current Black staff with decades of experience were the most likely to lament the lack of nodding, particularly among the younger generation of Black staffers. They told me nostalgic stories about how every Black person would nod in earlier periods, and some even spoke about critical interventions they made with other Black staff to teach them the rules about nodding and acknowledgment in Congress.

Cynthia, who has worked in Congress for over a decade for two Black members, told a story about how she taught a Black male to nod after he failed to acknowledge her in the hallways. She would later chide me during the interview for not knowing enough Black employees in Congress and relying on my office contacts to find people to interview rather than my own solid network of African American staff. Thomas, who worked as a staffer for a White senator in the 1970s and later on a Senate committee in the 1980s, did not know what the Black nod was when I asked him about the social practice. However, after I explained my observations, he sharply quipped, "Oh, you mean speaking!" Even if an African American did not know about the head nod, there was an assumption of acknowledgment and communication, either verbal or nonverbal, among African Americans. All of these Black elders in Congress maintain that nodding is simply something you do as a Black person to other Black people, especially when you are underrepresented in a particular space.

After decades of being in Congress, Jonathan, the chief of staff, believed he did not see the same level of participation of nodding among young Black staffers. He wondered if this new generation understood why these social practices were so vital for Black professionals:

> I have a friend of mine who works at the White House and assists in bringing in more minority candidates, people of color, into the administration. She wanted to have a conversation with me. I said, "Okay, come on up to 'the Hill.' We'll have it." I said, "Let's go to the House Floor. We're in recess, we'll just sit on the floor and talk." Which is something also that most people don't think that we would do. So, we're walking, and there were three young Black people walking toward us, two males and one female, just chatting, kinda, you know, coming. Both my friend and I stopped talking so we could sort of eye them and acknowledge them for who they are, to say, "Hello, how are you, good morning." They walked past us like we were not even there.

Jonathan's voice expresses equal parts amazement and disdain that he did not receive an acknowledgment from the young Black staffers. However, more important is the action that

Jonathan intended to take and how that reflects the underrepresented status of African Americans in Congress. Jonathan stopped his conversation with his colleagues to recognize African Americans, first by eye contact, and second with verbal communication. However, in this case, the interaction did not take place. Again, Jonathan notes he intended to acknowledge them just for who they are, young African Americans in a space where they are numerically rare. Here there is as a hint of racial pride of their accomplishments, and he later admits that he is more cognizant of these interactions with people of color than with Whites. This instance is also connected to his personal efforts to improve diversity in Congress; an issue that he says keeps him up at night. The purpose of this meeting with his colleague from the White House was to discuss ways to improve racial representation in the Obama administration; however, from his vantage point, the lack of nodding is a critical setback for those diversity initiatives.

The Black nod in many ways serves as a metaphor demonstrating the changes in the Black community on the Hill. Between the 1960s and 1990s, the number of Black legislative staff was extremely small; now, the group is several times larger, albeit still underrepresented. This shift in size changes the perceptions of race.[24] Racial paranoia represents the flipside of racial solidarity. Nodding among African Africans employees is a way to signal racial solidarity and convey a set of shared experiences and beliefs about the significance of race and racism. However, when an African American does not participate in the practice of nodding, perhaps by not reciprocating the gesture or by avoiding eye contact, other African Americans read this behavior as an indication that an African American does not share the same views and values. The uncertainty of the motives of Black non-nodding produces racial paranoia for those African Americans who do nod. In this instance, nodding facilitates the practice of boundary making among African American employees.[25] In informal conversations about the nod, African Americans would try to decipher why another African American would not acknowledge them, either by verbal or nonverbal communication; they would ultimately conclude that Black nonparticipants did not see the importance of racial cooperation and, to some extent, the circumstances that required it. Here the nod represents a certain disciplining of race, where Black staffers, particularly those who are older and more senior, insist that the only way to improve the status of African American staff on the Hill is to maintain a strong Black community. Thus, not nodding becomes an affront to those attempts at building power and community.

Racialized Professionalism

In this chapter, I have focused on why African Americans nod to one another in the halls of Congress. As I heard from other staffers over and over, and as many scholars confirm, the Black nod is a cultural gesture that communicates racial solidarity. It is certainly not specific to Congress. However, my interview data show that there is an additional layer of meaning attached to the nods that African Americans give one another when they walk through the Capitol. The impulse to nod is a manifestation of African American employees' attempts to survive and thrive in a workplace organized around Whiteness. The nod is encompassed and shaped by legislative work organized along racial lines, a history of racial subordination, and racial anxiety.

The nod on the Hill is imbued with layers of meaning and interpretation. For Monica, Cassie, Anthony, and Jordan, the preeminent meaning of the congressional Black nod is affirming the presence of other Blacks, in spite of being diluted in a

White-majority environment, in response to being ignored by White staff, and regardless of one's ideological or party affiliation. For Cassie and Jonathan, the nod is a performance of race that serves as a gestural equalizer and signal of racial authenticity. Given this importance, not nodding is interpreted on a micro level as a personal slight and on a macro level as an indicator of emerging fractures in shared Black identity across class and generational lines. Finally, Monica cites the strength of the nod as an adaptive strategy for affirming and reproducing Black solidarity without being so conspicuous that it is perceived as threatening to the White majority.

What comes across most clearly in interviews is how the Black nod is an adaptive strategy that renders African American staffers visible in an environment where they feel socially invisible. Given its value as an adaptive strategy that implies validation, recognition, and solidarity, when the nod is not initiated or reciprocated, Black staffers are not certain if this gestural absence is predicated on racism (from White staff) or on a fracturing of the shared Black identity (from other Black staff). What *is* certain is that these moments between stares and glances are fraught with racial anxiety; Black employees, in turn, deploy race as an explanation for both participation and nonparticipation.

In response to working in an environment organized by race, Black staff have developed a racialized professional identity.[26] Sociologist Celeste Watkins-Hayes developed the concept of racialized professionalism to describe how Black and Latino bureaucrats integrate race into their understanding and operationalization of work. I build on this concept, emphasizing how racialized dynamics in the workplace shape Black workers' professional identities. Through this racialized professional identity—and through the gestures that signify one's "membership in the club"—Black staff recognize social

divisions and prioritize the validation, respect, and acknowledgement of the work of fellow African Americans in Congress,
regardless of their political and occupational differences. The
Black nod is an external expression of Black staffers' racialized professional identity—an expression that is expected to
be given and sanctioned when not reciprocated. This deeper
understanding of the Black nod also reconceptualizes our
perception of Black congressional staffers as a group, mov-
ing us from viewing them as a powerless group to seeing them
with the potential to mobilize in subtle ways to enhance their
positions.[27] In the next two chapters, I build on this idea of a
racialized professional identity and describe how race informs
Black staffers' approach to their formal work responsibilities.

CHAPTER FOUR

A Seat at the Table

WHY RACIAL REPRESENTATION MATTERS

IN 1989 JACKIE PARKER was chair of the Senate Black Legislative Staff Caucus. The Senate committee on governmental affairs asked her to provide testimony at a hearing on applying federal workplace laws to Congress. She eloquently described the role Black staff play in the Senate, where they held less than 3 percent of senior policy positions: "With no Black members in the United States Senate, our caucus serves as a voice of Black America in the Senate on matters of national importance. It is not a role we choose, and it is not a position we cherish. We are not here as a result of any popular votes. Instead, we are a policy voice of Black America in the US Senate by default. We represent the descendants of people who did not come here by choice."[1]

Parker, who first arrived in 1979 when Senator Carl Levin hired her as his legislative assistant, spoke as a veteran of Capitol Hill. That was the same year Edward Brooke, the first African American popularly elected to Senate, left after two full terms.[2] During the intervening years, and for four years after she testified, there were no Black senators.[3] The absence of elected Black leadership in the Senate thrust upon her and her Black colleagues the collective responsibility to represent Black interests. Parker noted how this collective responsibility made their roles distinct from non-Black colleagues:

> For many years, we have struggled with our role in the Senate. We have walked a delicate balance. On the one hand, serving as political and policy advisors in a capacity identical to our non-Black staff colleagues. But at the same time, we have the responsibility to assure that the senators we serve are acutely aware of the impact of their decisions on the Black community—even in instances where those members are not significantly influenced by a Black voting population.[4]

Although Parker spoke about the dual role of Black staff decades ago, we still know surprisingly little about this group and their contributions. In this chapter, I ask what do Black staffers do and how are they different from White staffers?

We have explored who staffers are and how they get to the Hill; now, we are going to explore what these staffers do day after day. It is a lot. First and foremost, staffers are heavily involved in policy creation. They help lawmakers transform an idea into a proper legislative proposal, build support for these proposals among other offices and external stakeholders, track its movement through the committee system, and handle negotiations. Advancing from one stage to the next can take months or even years, and staffers are crucial in pushing the process forward.

Second, personal office staff also assist lawmakers in representing their constituents. Staffers are often the first to speak with constituents. They respond to their letters and phone calls, which means addressing many pleas for help. As one chief of staff explained, this could mean helping a constituent navigate the government bureaucracy to obtain their social security check or a passport. Additionally, staffers keep track of what is said in these correspondences, including the frustrations about occurrences in their districts and government, and they communicate it to their boss to guide lawmaking.

Third, staffers support lawmakers as leaders of a coequal branch of the federal government and monitor what the executive and judicial branches do. This oversight typically takes shape as committee hearings and investigations; appropriations; and the confirmation of judges and top-level executive branch officials. All this work requires staff acting behind the scenes, holding planning meetings, coordinating strategy, and providing advice and analysis.

Finally, staffers help run the legislative branch itself. Here, the work of staffers employed in committees and the offices of congressional leadership, like Speaker of the House and Senate majority leader, takes center stage. They help senior lawmakers strategize the best course of action, like determining how and when to advance legislation. There are also staffers employed in a range of nonpartisan offices like the Office of Legislative Counsel or the clerk of the House that provide legal expertise and administrative support to congressional offices.

As you can see, congressional staff do a lot. And this is not even an exhaustive list of everything they do. While there have been important scholarly conversations about the far-reaching influence of congressional staff on democratic governance, there has yet to be a closer look at what it means for this group to be overwhelmingly White and the implications for policymaking. One reason this omission persists is the implicit assumption that since a staffer works to achieve a lawmaker's political agenda, their own racial background does not matter. As such, there is a more robust scholarly conversation about how the race (along with gender and class identity) of a *law-maker* influences their policymaking, but relatively little about the influence of a lawmaker's staff.

Scholars who have focused on Congress for nearly a half century debated the merits of descriptive representation—a concept that refers to whether constituents benefit from having an elected official of the same racial or gender identity.[5] For example, numerous studies from political scientists demonstrate the variety of ways Black voters benefit from having a representative who looks like them.[6] What this research shows is that it matters who gets a seat at the table. Michael Minta found that Black lawmakers are more involved in committee hearings related to racial justice and social welfare policy than White lawmakers.[7] As he demonstrated, Black lawmakers took on the additional responsibilities of representing the Black community at large and used their oversight powers to enforce civil rights policies and encourage other political officials to direct their attention to issues confronting communities of color. Descriptive representation informs which policies are discussed, voted on, and implemented, and whether those policies are viewed as legitimate and fair.

Descriptive representation also matters for the numerous tasks that lawmakers do aside from casting votes because these other arenas are where Black lawmakers most explicitly work to advance minority interests. For instance, Christian Grose argued that descriptive representation matters most in what legislators do off Capitol Hill in how they deliver resources to constituents. "If we want to enhance substantive representation for Black constituents, and conceive of it as roll-call voting, then electing Black legislators is not important. However, if we want to enhance service and project delivery to Black constituents then descriptive representation in Congress is crucial."[8] Along those same lines, Richard Fenno identified how Black representatives serve as important role models for their Black constituents, outlining the symbolic value of descriptive representation.[9] To this end, political theorists like Lani Guinier and Jane Mansbridge emphasized how descriptive representation is crucial for enhancing the legitimacy of governing institutions and healing group mistrust held among marginalized communities.[10]

Ironically, while we know a lot about the benefits of descriptive representation among elected officials, we know considerably less about how description representation matters among their staff, who are similarly seated at the decision-making table and instrumental in facilitating these important conversations.

One noteworthy exception to this lacuna is the work of political scientists Cindy Rosenthal and Lauren Bell, who investigated the influence of women staffers on congressional committees.[11] They show that legislative staff from underrepresented backgrounds hold considerable power to influence legislative decision-making, particularly in areas that are not clearly racialized or gendered, and where lawmakers' interests are uncrystallized. For example, they analyzed the passage of the Consumer Bankruptcy Reform Act in the 105th Congress. Bankruptcy was broadly understood as an important economic issue, not a gender issue. Women staffers were instrumental in changing that faulty perception. Women staffers highlighted the negative consequences for women and their families if alimony and child support were allowed to be discharged in bankruptcy proceedings. As their research shows, descriptive representation matters among congressional staff too. Additionally, they point out that to engage in this work, women staffers need to be empowered in decision-making roles and have the trust and support of their lawmakers. Their work highlights the need for diverse representation among senior staffers.

As the preceding chapters show, race is determinative in deciding who gets to work on Capitol Hill and, once there, in which office and positions they will be employed. Race also determines how work gets done. That is, race shapes how staff provide critical advice and analysis to lawmakers in the creation of federal law and how they fulfill numerous other formal duties and informal responsibilities. If White staffers are overwhelmingly the only people in the room when decisions are made, it means that it is only their interests that are represented in federal lawmaking. Thus, this makes Congress not only a White space in a physical sense, but a location where Whiteness is enacted through policy.

In this chapter, I demonstrate how Black staffers push back against racial biases built into legislative work that is otherwise understood as business as usual on Capitol Hill. Black staffers use their position, expertise, and relationships with lawmakers to prevent discrimination in federal law and incorporate marginalized perspectives in legislative deliberations, work that I refer to as *inclusive policymaking*.[12] To be sure, this is work that all congressional staff should do, but don't. In my conversations with Black staffers and other staffers of color, they reflect on how their racial and gender identity impacts the work they do assisting our nation's leaders. Rather than emphasize how Black staffers do one just thing, I will show how this work exists on a continuum.

The Elephant in the Room

I spoke with Keisha for over an hour on the phone about her time in Congress. As a Black woman lawyer who worked for a White Republican, she had a lot to say. She explained how congressional staff, particularly those in mid- and senior-level positions, guide lawmakers' agendas: "To me, I am able to craft the senator's point of view." She emphasized that, although she held her own views, her recommendations were based on legal precedent and what made sense for her boss given his past voting record. "There's been plenty of times where I've stated, 'This is what I think. This is what I'm basing it on.' And he could just say, 'No.'" With that said, our conversation illuminated how much discretion staff hold because of the deliberative nature of lawmaking. As she explained, it mattered who was in the room as policy decisions were discussed, debated, and finalized. You need smart and knowledgeable staff for sure, but you also need diverse racial perspectives in the room as well.

Throughout our conversation, she continually brought up how she did not want to be pigeonholed in a racialized role. Yet the Whiteness of Capitol Hill, imbued in bodies and practices, thrust upon her the additional burden of confronting racism, which was not always obvious to her White peers. Keisha told me how she strategically used her position to challenge racist ideas in her office. She explained, "I, as an African American female, have an issue with any piece of legislation that has discriminatory practices in it, on it, around it, on its face." She recounted several instances where she fought against racist ideas in her office and how she strategically persuaded her senator to withdraw support from discriminatory legislation. "I really supported the agenda of my senator when I could. However, I don't think people understand how much power congressional staffers have. We inform the senators and congressmen of what is going on. They have barely enough time to think." As Keisha pointed out, lawmakers are extremely busy; their daily schedules are often broken down into fifteen-minute increments, and the topic from one meeting to the next is almost always different. Within this fast-paced environment, lawmakers lean on their staff, who have the time to carefully read through legislation and develop expertise on one or more issues.

One of the instances when Keisha used her expertise and personal judgment to guide her senator's policy agenda was on immigration. An immigration lobbying group petitioned her office to support upcoming legislation that would allow a special visa for Irish immigrants. As Keisha explained to me, she was personally opposed to this legislation because it would give preferential treatment. "I had to sit there and tell the senator, you can vote for this if you want, but you are putting Irish people in front of Black people, in front of the Indian person that has to wait seventeen years. You're saying that the Irish can decide to come to the United States and be offered this visa." This visa would allow, as Keisha described, Irish men and women to come to the United States with educational credentials similar to a high school degree, while other racial and ethnic group members would need more advanced degrees to obtain a visa. Deliberating with other senior staffers, Keisha passionately argued against supporting a racist double standard, telling them bluntly, "You are racist if you sign it." To further emphasize how this legislation would create preferential treatment for a select group, she continued, "If they have the Eritrean visa you better give it to them. If you don't want to be the Republican that's giving out every visa based on race, you better say no." While other senior staffers, who were White, pointed out that this was an important constituency in their state and many of their funders were Irish, Keisha held her ground, her position informed by both her legal training and her racial identity.

Ultimately, the senator deferred to Keisha's judgment and did not support the special visa. In subsequent meetings, Keisha was responsible for explaining to lobbyists why the senator could not support the proposed legislation. "I did not mind telling them every single problem I had with their deal. A lot of people didn't even realize that the status gave them preferential treatment." While Keisha was able to thwart an attempt to promote racially biased legislation, other staffers might not feel empowered to do so if they do not have a good relationship with their boss.

Although Keisha spoke at length about how she represented Black interests in her senator's policy agenda, she also framed this work as something more foundational: such efforts were just what it meant to be a good staffer, period. She, like many other Black staffers I interviewed, argued that representing Black interests and advocating for antidiscriminatory principles is not something only Black staffers should do, but it should be a requirement of all congressional staff.

Keisha talked about her guiding role as a staffer differently than George, a senior staffer in the same office, whom she recommended I interview. Keisha repeatedly mentioned her racial and gender identity and how it mattered; George, who is a White man, did not. To be sure, it is not that his race and gender did not matter, but rather as a White man he never had to think about it because the whole world is built presuming that his identity is at the center of everything. Just like Keisha, he expressed how staff can have a guiding role in policy formation. "Obviously it is not your name on the door, but as your responsibility and experience grow, some people take on roles not only of implementation but of guidance strategy." George was an experienced campaign operative who had worked for two senators, and it shows. What DC insiders like to call "guidance strategy" is a polite term for getting your boss to think the way you want them to think. He said an important part of his job as a senior staffer was to "speak up in a respectful and tactful way when your experience and judgment make you feel as if something is not the right approach the member should be taking and steer the member toward a better policy or political goal."

Keisha and George both agreed that congressional staffers have the power to influence policymaking but offered contrasting visions of what guidance strategy looked like. George imagined his political job as a game in which he tried to score points against the opposing team. He offered examples of how he helped his senator gain political advantage by attacking the Obama administration and other Republicans jockeying for his senator's seat. In contrast, Keisha, who was George's teammate, envisioned winning as enshrining fairness and equity in federal law. For her, those types of political victories would make her boss stand out on a crowded Republican field. Moreover, her professional identity was guided by her identity as a Black woman. In contrast, George rarely brought up race or gender in our interview. Nonetheless, they were both able to shape their senator's point of view in policy.

Speaking Up and Speaking Out

Keisha was not alone in disrupting the reproduction of White privilege in lawmaking decisions. Other Black staffers I spoke with actively worked to increase the rights and enhance the agency of marginalized groups in legislative deliberations. Black staffers' descriptive representation did not mean exclusive representation of Black interests. Instead, they argued that their racial and gender identity as Black men and women made them sensitive to difference and inequality of all kinds. To this end, when they deliberated with other congressional staffers about policy, they identified with other marginalized communities and sought to represent them as well.

Michelle worked as a senior staffer to a White Democratic senator during the 1990s. As a Black woman, she was one of the few female people of color to have a position of influence and authority in the Senate. During this time, Black staffers held only 1.4 percent of leadership positions like chiefs of staff, and only 4.6 percent of policy positions in the Senate.[13] She described how this context and her identity as a Black woman informed how she approached her job, which included overseeing policy deliberations with her staff and making final recommendations to her boss, a prominent senator. "I remember the late '90s—the Defense of Marriage Act [DOMA] was being debated. And there was a lot of consternation about it. There was a lot of debate about which amendments we would offer, knowing that DOMA was going to pass with overwhelming numbers." The legislation, which defined marriage for federal purposes as between a man and women and barred states from recognizing same-sex marriages, passed with the support of over 75 percent of lawmakers in the House and Senate. Still, there was a debate among Senate staff about which, if any, amendments their senator would offer that would mitigate the blow of the antigay legislation, which was almost certainly going to pass. "Part of that debate centered on a hate crimes bill that we had drafted, and . . . the Employment Non-Discrimination Act, which is the bill that targeted employment discrimination against gays and lesbians. And there were many and long debates among congressional staff about those two bills as amendments to DOMA."

In legislative deliberations, lawmakers and their staff make decisions about what is good policy and what is good politics, which oftentimes are not mutually exclusive. As Michelle described, the deliberations she had with her staff centered around whether or not to offer any antidiscrimination amendments, which everyone agreed was good policy, and what would be the larger political implications if the amendments failed, not only for her boss, but the LGBTQ community more broadly. "We were thinking about what message we were sending—if the votes were too low, would we be damaging those issues going forward? All of those things—was it the right time to do that?"

On the eve of the passage of the notoriously antigay bill, which the Supreme Court ruled unconstitutional in 2013 and Congress fully repealed in 2022, Michelle described a chaotic behind the scenes filled with conflicting opinions and no clear consensus on what to do. However, as the most senior staffer in the room, she had the ability to end the rancorous debate:

> I remember sitting in those conversations and having people make the arguments about whether or not it was time. And at one point it really did just hit me that in just about forty years and less than that before, people had been having those debates around the Civil Rights Act of '64 and '65. And those debates were about me as a woman, about me as an African American. And at some point you have to determine that you're going to push forward . . . and I also had a strong sense of where my boss would be. And I remember just deciding, "I'm not going to sit here and debate this issue anymore. I'm going back to my office and getting ready for the debate on the floor. And [we] should talk to [the senator] about why we have to move forward." And I did. And we did.

The amendment that Michelle successfully persuaded her boss to take up did not get a majority vote, but in her opinion, "it was a major step forward for that piece of legislation." Michelle reiterated how she saw her identity influencing her professional identity by stating, "It was my own view and my own understanding of history and my personal experience that really helped me reach a conclusion about what was possible and what had to be done." Similar to Keisha, Michelle found herself in the exact situation that George described above, strategizing with other legislative staffers to develop the best policy recommendation for her boss. To be clear, Michelle did not see herself as a racial representative; in fact, she insisted, like many White staffers, that her role was limited to supporting her boss's vision. She stated, "I felt that my responsibility was to the senator and to driving forward the agenda that he was setting." However, in the extended quote above, we see that race and gender were still important in how she understood policy issues. More importantly, in her capacity as a senior staffer, Michelle had the ability to act on that understanding, ending the conversation among the staffers and making the final policy recommendation to the senator.

Other staffers of color I interviewed, as well as a few White women, similarly described why descriptive representation was important in legislative deliberations, particularly in rooms that are filled with White heterosexual men. Julia, a White Republican, proclaimed, "I really viewed it as my role, I jokingly say, as a woman to raise my hand and tell them how bad their ideas were." Julia was candid about her experiences working for White Republican men. She had worked as one of the highest-ranking women in the House Republican leadership, where she had the personal attention of senior lawmakers. Congressional leaders like the Speaker of the House or Senate majority leader have their own staffs, often housed in stately offices in the Capitol, to help them manage Democratic and Republican caucuses. "When you work in a rank-and-file office, in a personal office, you really have to be careful because it is your job to advance that member of Congress's agenda, and your personal politics cannot play too much into it. When you work for the Republican leadership, it was my job to advise them on what was overall best for our leadership team, our conference, and frankly for our party." She often found herself as the dissenting voice against the more conservative perspectives. "It was tough because the reality is the conference is made up of White men who are pro-life and antigay, mostly. Those are my two issues where I would disagree with the majority of the conference." Nonetheless, she found herself as a staffer in a leadership office being the contrarian. "If they were trying to advance something I thought was a bad move politically, at least there was one person in the room telling them it was a bad idea."[14] In many ways, Julia highlights the limitations of congressional staff to influence policymaking. As her experiences demonstrate, members of Congress still have the final say, at least on some matters, in policy and political conversations. However, descriptive representation among staff is important, even if it does not always translate to clear policy wins. Most legislative deliberations happen behind closed doors, between lawmakers and their staff. Descriptive representation among staff ensures that multiple perspectives will be heard and adds legitimacy to a process that is not easily observed by the public. As Julia put it, her presence guaranteed that at least one dissenting view would be articulated.

The Congressional Hispanic Staff Association has documented the persistent underrepresentation of Latino staff in Congress, particularly in senior positions. In their 2020 report, "Still Underrepresented," they found "that there were no Latino [committee] staff directors in the Senate and almost no Democratic Latino staff on the three top Senate committees. In the House, Latino chiefs of staff would have to increase fivefold to represent the nearly one in five Americans of Latino descent."[15] This persistent underrepresentation of Latino staff on Capitol Hill translates to legislative deliberations where few staffers have firsthand knowledge of Latino communities, even as they have the responsibility of making policy decisions that will affect their lives. Alejandra, a Latina staffer in the House, stated, "I think, ultimately, the conversations that are being held in Capitol Hill would be a lot different if it wasn't for our input, just because having a person with a background the same as your constituents and things that other individuals might not acutely be aware of or not as sensitive, you can bring it up in those conversations."

Alejandra's background growing up in an immigrant community was, not surprisingly, pertinent for her work as a legislative assistant covering immigration and border security. She brought up as an example a discussion about a program called Secure Communities that mandates fingerprinting of everyone in prison, which consequently leads to the deportation of undocumented immigrants. Alejandra did not oppose the overall aim of the policy. "It's good, right, because you want to make sure that people who are here are not threatening communities, and it's important that you do a fingerprint run, and if these individuals are here unlawfully and they're committing crimes, of course, go ahead and deport them, by all means. I want my communities to be safe."

However, her experiences growing up in an immigrant community (alongside her professional expertise in border security, education, and labor) were crucial in leading her to understand how this policy could have unintentional consequences and make communities less safe. "But what happens in some states is that when it comes to domestic violence, there's mandatory arrests for both parties—the victim and the perpetrator. So as a Latina and coming from an immigrant background, I'm more acutely sensitive to that because I can see how to a person who does not come from an immigrant background, it's like, 'Oh, this is good, you're fingerprinting everybody and you're catching all the bad people,' but then when you have laws like this or mandatory arrests, victims of domestic violence might be less forthcoming in reporting abuse. So, coming from that background and seeing members of your community being scared, you can bring that up to the table, and that's a consideration that other people didn't have." As Alejandra explained, diverse representation is necessary for helping policymakers think through the intricacies of complex issues and identifying the negative effects that might result from their decision-making. In short, diverse staff representation helps to reduce the chances that a policymaker will do harm while they try to do good.

The Woman Behind the Curtain

Karen worked for a Black representative who had a hands-on approach toward policy. She pointed out that, although he had a stellar reputation as smart and independent, he was a busy member of Congress who still needed to rely on his staff to execute his agenda. To this end, Karen explained her job as a senior staffer "as the eyes and ears for the member." As his eyes and ears, she would bring pertinent matters to his attention that he might otherwise overlook because of his busy schedule. Beyond keeping her lawmaker informed, like all the other staffers we've talked about so far, she presented ideas and options to help guide and define her boss's legislative agenda.

During Karen's five-year stint working for her boss, a senior Democrat representative, she split her time working for his personal office and handling his committee work. Her boss was a subcommittee chairman for a top committee in the House, making his schedule even busier than a typical member. As a subcommittee chairman he could hold hearings on various legislative proposals as well as conduct investigations on matters that fell within the subcommittee's jurisdiction. This broad power and wide discretion only added to his busy schedule and further empowered staffers like Karen to take a leading role in guiding their boss's agenda—not only his personal agenda, but also his committee priorities. As she explained her role, "With respect to hearings, that's what's wonderful about being a chair—being able to craft and have hearings on the issues that you think are important. It was an opportunity, really, to move somebody's agenda along. And, you know, [he] gets so busy. More often than not, it was we who brought ideas to him."

One of the ideas Karen and her staff brought to her boss was to hold a hearing about credit scores—which determine a consumer's creditworthiness—to learn about how these scores are produced. "Oftentimes, minorities have lower credit scores, and people don't know what goes into them and what the methodology is, what factors they use. We decided to have a hearing on that issue and brought it to [his] attention." After her boss signed off on the hearing, Karen and other staffers did everything to bring their idea to life:

> So we brought in all of the crediting agencies as well as some private sector privacy people. For the majority of witnesses we would write the hearing memo and focus the hearing in a particular direction. So we often had an idea from the very beginning about what we wanted to get out of the hearing, to the point of not only preparing questions for [the chairman] to elicit certain responses, but we also put together potential questions and share them with the staff of the Democratic committee. Sometimes they love them because that's less work for them.

Karen's description offers a behind-the-scenes look at what it takes to put on a congressional hearing. Staffers play a leading role in facilitating this process, from idea generation and witness selection to writing questions and scripting the hearing to (hopefully) creating the viral moments that can be circulated in the news media and on social media platforms. These hearings are important because they have agenda-setting powers, which can start new national discussions, change policy, and redirect resources. These oversight hearings also allow lawmakers, especially members of color, to hold other political actors accountable. If a hearing goes well, members of Congress receive a lot of noteworthy attention from media and among voters. Lawmakers get all the credit for punchy statements and probing questions to witnesses that are most times written by their staff. Staffers rarely get credit for this work in public, nor does the public even know they are the ones doing the work. We do not even notice their presence in these hearings, where they are seated right behind lawmakers on the committee dais.

One moment stuck out to Karen in the years since she organized the hearing about credit scores. "I'll never forget: we mentioned to [my boss] that you can get a free credit report each year. He didn't even know that was out there. One of the things he said in the opening statement at the hearing is that he also learned a lot about this, too." As she explained, part of organizing the hearing meant educating the member on the ins and outs of an issue. "One of the things we did for [him] was to go to different agencies and pull his credit for him so he could see it and get an idea and see how often the scores from different agencies are not even close together. It was defi-nitely a learning experience for him." Karen was very modest and showed considerable deference to her boss. However, in actuality, she played a more consequential role. She was the woman behind the curtain, orchestrating the hearing from start to finish. This includes educating her boss on important consumer issues, which he was in charge of.

As Karen's career experiences point out, Black staff repre-sentation is also important in the offices of Black lawmakers. While members of the Congressional Black Caucus, commonly referred to as the conscience of the Congress, have a clear antiracist agenda, staffers like Karen are crucial in helping to define these broad interests. They play a decisive role in determining which issues get congressional attention and educating their bosses on topics that might go unnoticed and that have clear implications for communities of color.

Representing All Constituents

Aside from their responsibilities as policy experts, legislative staffers also respond to the needs of their constituents. Constituent work is mostly done in district and state offices, however, legislative staffers in Washington, DC, also interact with constituents. In Washington, DC, constituent services include responding to constituent mail and phone calls; arranging congressional and White House tours; administering internships; providing bureaucratic guidance; and meeting with constituents. These activities represent core responsibilities of Congress and are important for lawmakers' reelection. Previous research demonstrates that constituent services is a medium through which minority lawmakers can disproportionately serve communities of color.[16] However, staffers are deeply involved in this process as well. I found that Black staffers help ensure that the concerns of communities of color are attended to in Congress.

Constituent services was an integral part of Karen's job. "As staffers, we were responsible for reading and responding to those letters that came in and touched on our issue areas. That would allow us, actually, to be able to understand what the constituents' views are and about the way things should be." In her office, everyone, no matter their seniority, was responsible for responding to constituent mail. In contrast, in most other offices it is junior staffers, like staff assistants and legislative correspondents, who reply to these letters. As Karen explained, responding to constituent mail, more generally, allows lawmakers and their staff to know the concerns of the people they represent intimately. "Constituents often write in, but what often happens is that constituents write in a response to something like a bill, not necessarily with a new idea, and you get to know what their priorities are and what is important to them." However, she added that that process was key for serving the interests of overlooked groups. "There was this feeling that we were representing all the constituents in the district, of course, but at the same time there was a particular point of making sure we are representing those who are often underrepresented and who don't always have the strongest voice for themselves." Karen's relationship with constituents was key to guiding her boss's agenda. "If I brought a suggestion to his attention about, for example, including something or other, oftentimes it was because I had had an individual meeting with a constituent who raised an issue that he might not be aware of. So, of course, making sure that he is aware of what the constituents say is important." Although staff are supposed to represent all constituents and their interests, it does not necessarily mean that all staff do that, as several Black staffers pointed out to me. "For me, there was a lot of pride and feeling of commitment, whereas sometimes people let things slide."

Deidre, who I mentioned in a previous chapter, worked for a White lawmaker as legislative counsel but described her role as a racial broker, connecting her White boss to the communities of color he represented. "He has a high Hispanic and high Latino population, and even a part of our new district, he has a decent African-American constituency. So my goal has been and still is to try to shape his priorities, to reflect all of his—all of his constituency, especially those that are—that

I think—I wouldn't say he's—I wouldn't say he's not aware of them. But they don't have as much of a voice, as some of the other constituencies in our district." To this end, she told me how she strategized with their district staff to get her boss in front of constituents of color, who otherwise might get overlooked. "My goal as I work with the district staff, right now first and foremost, is to get him in front of those audiences. To form that relationship and create a forum where they can let him know what their issues and concerns are."

While Deidre strove to be an interlocutor for her White boss and the communities of color that he represented, part of that work meant convincing her coworkers, who were almost all White, to share this same vision. "I have great relationships with the folks in my office. I do get a little upset with some of them, because I feel like we are an afterthought—when I say 'we,' I mean the constituency that I'm trying to represent." As Deidre told me, her boss loved her in the office and sought out her candid perspectives; however, she disclosed that her chief of staff had more influence to define the legislative agenda and keep their priorities focused on those who already had a loud voice. "Sometimes we are an afterthought, and our focus is so driven on the folks who have our boss's ear, so to speak. And they have this ear because they were friends with him, or they have the money. I feel like sometimes our focus is on what they want. We pay too much attention to it!" Deidre's experience trying to present a more inclusive vision for constituent services points to how political agendas are negotiated—not merely established by the lawmaker, but rather evolved, via the lawmaker's own beliefs alongside the influences of senior staffers and others around them. Sometimes a staffer can prompt new ideas and perspectives that the lawmaker wouldn't otherwise see; other times, a staffer can stop new ideas from reaching the member.

Jonathan, a Black chief of staff, believed that diverse representation among congressional staff mattered when his constituents visited their DC office. Echoing Deidre's sentiment about money and politics, he explained that it is often easier for lobbyists and consultants to get a meeting with lawmakers and congressional staff than Black and Brown citizens. He said, "When Delta [airlines] comes down, they've always got a meeting." However, he made it a point in his hectic and busy schedule to make time for underrepresented groups from local communities in his district. "When all the youth groups come down, if I'm here, I always take time to talk to them because I want them, number one, to know that I'm here and also know that we're going to be helpful." Meeting with constituents is not one of the top job responsibilities of a chief of staff, but for Jonathan, this work, which could be easily ignored or passed along to a junior staffer, was important. As one of the few Black chiefs of staff, meeting with a youth of color had multiple meanings. It signaled how in Congress there are people of color in influential positions and that they are committed to serving the needs of historically overlooked groups.

Racial representation in Congress is important for many reasons; however, one of the most significant effects of increasing minority representation in staff positions is that it could possibly increase faith in our democratic institutions. Black staffers pointed out what most of us believe about Congress, that wealthy and well-connected individuals have an easier time accessing lawmakers than ordinary voters, especially those from historically marginalized communities. However, they challenged business as usual by making the legislature more accessible and responsive to Black and Brown constituents. This work for a staffer might be writing a thoughtful response to a constituent inquiry, organizing forums back home where citizens could speak directly to their elected officials, or making a hometown visitor's trip to the Capitol memorable. These acts may sound small, but they are significant. This work chips away at the political cynicism that is all too common today and can help improve the negative image of Congress.

It's Not My Name on the Door

Black and White staffers alike often told me, "It's not my name on the door." It was a common refrain, one that expressed a staffer's allegiance to their elected boss. They said this to newcomers to explain how legislative offices operated as political enterprises for lawmakers.[17] And they said this to themselves to manage their emotions and the feelings of disappointment that would arise when their boss inevitably ignored their recommendation and made a decision that they disagreed with. Walter, a Black staffer, said as much to me at the outset of our conversation. "One of the things that is paramount for congressional staffers is that, at the end of the day, our name is not on the door; it is the name of the congressman on the door, and we have to check our attitude and do what we need to do." However, this was also their way of informing me that they were not pursuing their own agendas within the office. Staffers would offer this response when I asked about how they influenced their lawmaker's political and policy agendas and the significance of their own racial and gender background. When I first asked about the impact of race on their work, Black staffers, no matter their political affiliation, would provide a race-neutral job description of their work. Additionally, they were pushing back against racist narratives that their work was about exclusively helping Black people. However, after deeper probing, these staffers would admit that their background inevitably influenced their jobs. This, of course, did not mean that they were pursuing their own agendas; instead, they recognized the importance and necessity of diverse perspectives in the legislative process. Walter exhibited this pattern of double talk. In our phone interview, he reiterated how his job as a staffer was to support his lawmaker's agenda. He then later stated how his social identity as a Black gay man was pertinent for how he advised his lawmaker.

Walter started his congressional career as a staff assistant for a senior Black lawmaker from the South. After two years, he took on a policy role as a legislative assistant in the office. One of the projects he worked on was a program that championed minority contracting within the federal government. As he described it, these programs were increasingly coming under legal assault from equal opportunity opponents. He worked with stakeholders to build a predicate, evidence that proves that discrimination exists and that these programs are necessary. Citing the progress he made on this front, he said, "It is one of the things I am most proud of from my time on the Hill."

At this point, I was unclear about how this assignment came about and if this work might have developed from his own initiative. I followed up by asking if he could provide any examples of work that he initiated that supported the congressman's agenda. "Not really. As I said earlier, our job is to carry forward his priorities, not necessarily ours. If they align, that's great, but it is not my job to bring forward things that I care about or to try to make the congressman care about them too. We both care about a lot of the same issues and together thought many things were important." Moments later, however, Walter revealed how his social background was pertinent to how he advised his new boss, a White congressman.

Walter transitioned to working for a moderate White Democrat after five years working for a Black congressman. In this new office, he held a senior position, which gave him more influence. When I asked Walter what past experiences shaped

how he did his job, he replied, "Being a Black man is something that informs how I advise my boss. Being a Black gay
man makes me even more sensitive to indifference and intol-
erance." He continued by underscoring how his social identity
allowed him to recognize the importance of human difference:
"Understanding that people are different and that we all have
something to bring to the table; recognizing others' strengths
can enable you to do your job better and be a better person."
He offered an example of how his racial identity influenced
how he advised his new boss.

> We were offering an amendment that would add money to
> the COPS program, which is a federal program that allows
> localities to hire additional police officers and buy equip-
> ment and things of that nature. In this new Republican
> Congress, if we are going to spend money, we have to pay
> for it. So, the options we had before us were to take it from
> DOJ [Department of Justice] or from the Census. Hav-
> ing worked in my previous office, I am very sensitive to
> how important the Census is to our community as Afri-
> can Americans. The count helps us to know how much
> resources are needed, where those resources are going,
> etc. So, because of my sensitivity and knowing where that
> money was going to come from, the congressman under-
> stood, and we did not go for that amendment.

Furthermore, Walter's work was influenced not only by his
racial identity but also by his sexuality. He told his new boss,
a White heterosexual congressman, that he was gay on the
House Floor. They were having a conversation about their
weekend plans when he unexpectedly opened up about his sexuality. Walter barely remembered the moment, it was unevent-
ful, a blur, he told me. "He was totally fine with it. It really
was no big deal." After that moment, however, his sexuality

did inspire new conversations with his boss. "I remember that, after having a conversation with the congressman about my own sexuality, we had a conversation about why he cannot be a supporter of the big issues, like marriage equality, but wanted to look for other ways to be supportive. When those opportunities come up—being able to cosponsor legislation, for example—those are bills that I definitely champion for and try to assuage any concerns he might have about how that might be perceived back home." His boss represented a conservative district, and being a leading proponent of LGBTQ rights could diminish his prospects for reelection. Instead, his boss found ways to be an ally, albeit in the background, in part, because of his relationship with Walter. However, his boss's advocacy for LGBTQ rights was also predicated on Walter's own initiative, with him finding opportunities for his boss to support antibullying and nondiscrimination acts, for example.

Stating "it's not my name on the door" arguably meant something different when said by Black staffers, who walk a tightrope in a White-dominated institution. Their position is precarious. This phrase obscures the influence of congressional staff and the importance of descriptive representation among them. It allowed them to show considerable deference and dedication to their lawmakers who, for very practical reasons, need to be seen as the person in charge by voters and various stakeholders, even though, in practice, they might have been quite distant from the day-to-day operations in their own offices. Additionally, it allowed them to demonstrate their own commitment to professionalism and excellence. When Black staffers in the offices of White lawmakers reached out to overlooked constituent groups, namely Black and Latino constituents, it is an example of descriptive representation, but it is also something that all staffers should do. Yet this common refrain minimized their own contributions to the lawmaking process and downplayed the larger significance of having Black staffers, and other staffers of color, in influential positions.

It is worth noting why saying "it's not my name on the door" is necessary for Black staffer. It suggests the need for them to demonstrate their value and defend their position of influence within a White-dominated workplace. It allows them to affirm how they have rightfully earned their professional success because of their expertise and commitment to service, not their race. Moreover, it shields them from accusations of racial activism, which critics inside and outside their office might frame as improper and illegitimate.

Cole, a legislative director, felt the pressure of being the only Black person in the room and the tension between being a voice for his race and an effective staffer. "You feel responsibility. I do think that. I speak to constituents all the time and a lot of times they do not have a seat at the table and we talk about my job as a legislative director is to make sure that they have a seat at the table." At the same time he believed that "the challenge as a Black staffer is to be effective for your boss and yet retain your ability to be marketable in the private sector or in other government positions." Put simply, Cole did not think it was possible for him as a Black staffer to always advocate for racial justice and not be marginalized.

Cole perceived a stigma associated with staffers working on racialized issues, and he shaped his policy portfolio to be more mainstream. For example, although he was interested in foreign policy with a personal interest in the Caribbean and Africa, he gravitated toward foreign policy focused in other sectors of the world like Europe and Asia. "I think I did probably too good of a job staying away from those issues and focusing on other things because I didn't want to be stereotyped as the Black guy that handles the Black things." He avoided these issues because he suspected that Black staffers, and even Black members, that primarily worked on Black issues would have diminished career prospects on and off the Hill. "How does a member of Congress, or as a staffer representing a member, advocate for access to resources for individuals for communities that aren't performing economically? If we invest five dollars in the Northeast and it generates a twenty-dollar return, but if we invest five dollars in the Southeast we might only get $5.60 in economic return. There is an opportunity cost. And it's always a challenge to advocate for that lower return."

Cole was candid in his assessment of the Washington landscape and the challenges associated with representing marginalized interests. "I am not trying to dance my way around it, but what I am saying is that in a political environment where economic returns really dominate the priorities of members of Congress, one can find themselves marginalized rather quickly if they are advocating for disparate communities—for investment in disparate communities where the economic return isn't necessarily immediate." He imagined, "If I walk in and I am a firebrand in a room about WIC [Special Supplemental Nutrition Program] or I am a firebrand in the room about minority-owned businesses, people are going to look at me like, you know, there you go. He's just advocating—he only sees that one African American agenda. And that doesn't play. It just doesn't."[18] Cole believed that representing marginalized interests required a certain level of interpersonal skill. "This is a career. These are communities and circles that you are going to spend your entire professional life in, matriculating through, and the whole point is to present to other individuals—to persuade individuals to agree with your perspective. The challenge is there to relate with individuals that don't have your economic agenda on their front burner or even on their back burner."

With work experiences in both houses of Congress, Cole understood that "nine times out of ten you realize in this business it is not about being the best. It is about being the best positioned." He thought carefully about how to position himself in his career, to advocate for racial issues, and for future career opportunities.

His candid comments highlight how at least some staffers are always working with one foot out the door, trying to figure out what happens next, whether it's on Capitol Hill or in the private sector. Observing the ascendancy of then Senator Obama and continuing to work in Congress during the Obama administration, he thought he could best position himself by avoiding racialized issues. In the Obama era, there were still clear differences between what White staffers and Black staffers could do. White staffers advocating for and representing White interests is the norm. It is expected, uncontroversial, and a pathway for success. The opposite is true for Black staffers, and Black professionals more broadly. Sociologist Sharon Collins found that Black executives who manage "services directed at, disproportionately used by, or concerned with Blacks" experience limited mobility compared to those in mainstream positions that did not focus on any particular constituency or consumer in the private or public sector.[19] Moreover, she documented that these jobs are more likely to be downsized or cut while mainstream positions are more likely to be expanded or remain unchanged. In the Obama era, Cole did not see how he, as a Black professional, could be successful working on just "Black issues," nor were there many templates to suggest that he was wrong.

Inevitably, by virtue of being Black in a White-dominated place, Black staffers end up advocating for the needs of the Black community more than White staffers do, but how they do so, and how adamantly they do so, varies widely. Their approach was based upon how they understood racial issues, as well as their own personal experiences and what they

thought they needed to do to get ahead as a Black professional.[20] What's more, as we have seen, Black staffers advo-
cated for marginalized interests more broadly, exhibiting
an intersectional approach to legislative work, and what I
describe as *inclusive policymaking*.

Reifying Whiteness in Lawmaking

Throughout this chapter, I have shown why descriptive representation is so important in congressional offices. Staffers of
color play a pivotal role in highlighting the unique concerns
and needs of marginalized communities from which they
come. This matters because legislative work is not always
determined by the clear-eyed vision of lawmakers, but rather
it is the culmination of numerous debates and discussions
among them and their staff. Descriptive representation helps
ensure that multiple perspectives will be heard in policymaking decisions, which is ultimately what we want in a democratic
institution like Congress. My hope is that in future discussions
about who gets a seat at the table in our political institutions
that our conversations grow to include the professionals who
assist and guide the men and women we elect. Whereas in this
chapter I focused on descriptive representation in lawmakers'
personal offices and congressional committees, spaces that are
recognizable to the public, I want to conclude by briefly highlighting why representation matters in other types of congressional offices.

Susan was one of approximately forty attorneys who worked
for the House Office of Legislative Counsel. I am guessing
most readers have never heard of this office, but it is highly
influential and a crucial resource for lawmakers and their
staff. The office, which is just over a century old, helps lawmakers and staff, the majority of whom have no legal training,

draft legislation. They tell lawmakers what they can and cannot legally do, making them pivotal actors in the creation of federal law. As Susan succinctly described, these lawyers are "the crafters and the ghost writers of the laws that the members will introduce into the House and Senate." Accordingly, because legislative counsel works with every office, their work is "nonpartisan, impartial, and confidential."[21]

During her time in legislative counsel, Susan was the only Black attorney within its ranks. You might be tempted to think that racial and gender representation should not matter in a nonpartisan office, an office that is guided by fidelity to the law; and yet, as critical race theory scholars point out, there is nothing neutral about the law.[22] As Susan put it, "When those crafters and ghost writers and experts only look like they are White men, then there's a perception that is relayed across the body that only a White man, disproportionately, can recommend something that is legal and devoid of criticisms." She highlights the symbolic importance of racial diversity among legislative staff, particularly those employed in nonpartisan offices, as essential for ending the normalization of Whiteness in legislative work.

When Susan settled into her position, she looked up her predecessors. She was incensed to see that over the office's hundred-year history, there had only been five or so Black attorneys. The lack of racial diversity is likely due to a confluence of factors, such as the lack of turnover. Although most staffers enter and exit members' personal offices within a couple of years, Susan described legislative counsel as "an office from which you could legitimately retire." She added, "Most of the attorneys would stay for, really, fifteen to twenty-five years." There is also, as there is across professions, a gatekeeping that is, because of systemic racism, inevitably—even if not always intentionally—discriminatory.[23] The lawyers currently in the group (nearly all White, and elite) guard access to this prestigious club, and they recruit from the places they know best and from the people they know best: elite law schools with overwhelmingly White student populations. And so the cycle repeats itself. But another factor is also at play. This office of legal ghostwriters is largely out of public view, and their vital work is largely unknown. Therefore, there is no public pressure to integrate the office, unlike in the offices of most elected representatives. And those on Capitol Hill have tacitly accepted the association between Whiteness and legal expertise. Whatever the reasons, the office remained entirely White save for Susan.

It had been almost ten years since her initial interview with legislative counsel when I spoke to Susan about her congressional career, which included numerous other positions on Capitol Hill. She had gotten the job after a grueling interview process. At one point, she found herself at a roundtable with over twelve attorneys, her future colleagues—all of them White. While most of the interview was similar to other legal interviews she had done—questions about her background and where she sees herself in her future—two elements stood out, even a decade later. "I remember being the only person of color in the room out of the people filing in and out; I remember being one of a handful of women in the room also." These racialized and gendered dynamics increased the pressure for an already high-stakes interview where she sat "at the head of this interview table," where a cast of all White lawyers cycled in and out of the room "firing questions," "collectively interviewing you and determining whether or not you can stand up under pressure, how poised are you, how responsive are you, how nervous are you."

For most of the interview, Susan felt the scrutiny and evaluation she received was fair and routine until they asked a "question that they probably should not have asked, but they did ask." They asked "how I would feel about working on the Fourteenth Amendment?" Ratified after the Civil War, this amendment established citizenship for Black men and women and guaranteed them equal protection before the law. To be clear, what they were asking her was if she could work for a racist lawmaker who sought to undermine civil rights law. She replied to them, "While I might not agree with the underlying substance of the policy, your job as a lawyer is to craft the product in a manner that is legal and constitutional and consistent with existing law." Stating explicitly, "It's not my job to necessarily weigh in on, you know, my personal feelings," which mattered in legislative counsel because, if hired, she would be assigned to work on any number of legal issues and for any member, including someone who could express openly racist views. For this reason, she could not also have had any past employment with a partisan office, which would be an obvious indication of her political leanings. However, as she told me, "any lawyer who's a good lawyer knows that while you may disagree with the proposal, it's really your job to defend the client." More critically, sociologist Wendy Leo Moore asserts that "thinking like a lawyer requires a manner of thinking that acquiesces to a White normative framework and simultaneously facilitates the invisibility of Whiteness by precluding forms of argumentation that seek to identify the power and privilege that mark it."[24]

Susan felt that the committee was not only trying to decipher if she was a good lawyer but if, as a Black attorney, she would be impartial. She knew that this was not a standard question that legislative counsel asked lawyers they were recruiting because a "former coworker told me later on that they weren't supposed to ask that question." She intimated that they were trying to get "any personal perception or feelings that I would have, of course, with the Fourteenth Amendment that gave equal opportunity to Blacks, right? And as the only Black person in the room, it, of course, had other ramifications." As Susan recounts, when legislative counsel hired her, they were trying to maintain their impartiality and ascertain if she could do the same. However, impartiality might also mean working to uphold White supremacy.

Susan believed, "Congress should be representative of the country it serves and the staffers in Congress should be representative of the country it serves." She added, "You cannot have a homogeneous congressional office and purport to be representative of the country as a whole. And that stands even more so for those nonpartisan offices." She provided a clear example of why racial representation matters in nonpartisan offices and how the dominance of White attorneys in legislative counsel facilitates the reproduction of Congress as a White space. "It replicates a status quo in that you're in a position where you're essentially telling every member office in which you come into contact, and every committee with which you come into contact—these people don't turn over, the experts, they look this way, and this is their background." She emphasized that "as an office that sets the standard, because it does [not] really turn over, it's even more critical that it be a diverse representation of the country as a whole."

Politics gets in the way of having a representative congressional workplace—however, Susan averred that should not be the case in offices that are not supposed to be nonpolitical. In those spaces, more than others, they should exhibit our democratic and legal principles. Like other Black staff I interviewed, Susan had her own ways of trying to change Congress as a White space. She kept a detailed database of staffers of color

that she could quickly utilize if someone asked her for a recommendation for a vacancy. However, in her capacity as a staff
attorney in legislative counsel, perhaps her most important
contribution was the simple act of being there. Her presence
was a subversive act, and, as she put it, one that helped challenge the long-held association between Whiteness and legal
expertise in the Capitol.

CHAPTER FIVE

Black Capital

FIXING THE PROBLEM FROM THE INSIDE

KELLY, WHO HAD BEEN chief of staff for several House Republicans, had seen over and over how White Congress is from one
session to the next. "Every couple of years there's this thing that
comes out through some media outlet up here and it really does
happen every two years or so, where someone is studying the
number of Black staffers, and somebody comes out and says
there is this abysmal number of Blacks staffers." She was featured in one of those articles in the early 2000s, but almost a
decade later, the problem persisted without any meaningful
actions from House leadership. "I can remember last spring,
when I left here, a bunch of people emailing me that Speaker
Pelosi and then Leader Boehner had entered into some type of
agreement to do some kind of push, some outreach, to increase
the number of Black staffers. And I can remember, because I was
at home at the time, I wasn't working. I can remember reaching
out to a couple of people offering to be helpful, saying that I had
been the only African American chief of staff for the entire time
I had been with my former boss and that this is an issue, this is

a problem, let me know how I can be helpful. Zip. From either side. I didn't expect Boehner to get back to me, right, but nothing from the Democrats either, so it's a problem across the board."

Black chiefs of staff, like Kelly, are uniquely positioned to help Congress diversify its workforce. In their own offices, they control who gets hired and promoted. Additionally, they provide advice and referrals to other lawmakers and congressional leadership about how to best attract and retain people of color in staff positions.

I interviewed five other Black chiefs of staff, and two deputy chiefs of staff, who worked for Black and White lawmakers in both chambers, about the racial demographics of their offices. They all bragged about having some of the most racially diverse offices on Capitol Hill. I asked them about what they did differently to produce this outcome. Black chiefs of staff focused on creating a more inclusive workplace in general—by hiring the best people and by trying to correct for systemic and longstanding exclusions. That benefited Black people, for sure, since they were more likely to be hired than they would have been by a White chief of staff, presumably. But it also benefited women of all backgrounds and men of color.

In this chapter, I focus on the various strategies Black staffers use to make the congressional workplace more racially inclusive. I also illuminate Black staffers' collective work to bring public attention to legislative inequality. I spotlight their behind-the-scenes efforts to hold lawmakers accountable for who they hire.

Diversifying Capitol Hill

Jonathan, a Black chief of staff and an ardent nodder, was outspoken about his interest in helping Black professionals get staff jobs on the Hill. When he first approached his boss about diversifying their office, his boss, a White Democrat, said, "Whatever you do, make sure it's quality over quantity." Jonathan agreed. "I actually appreciated that," he said, "because that's what I do. 'I'm like, yes, quality over quantity, but if I bring in quality, it will increase quantity.' " Jonathan elaborated, "If all we're doing is hiring people who are unqualified and unable to do the job; that makes my challenge even harder because now I have to prove that there are people that actually can do the job and who should be promoted."

It took Jonathan more than a decade to achieve a majority-minority staff in his office. He used the high turnover among congressional staff as an opportunity to bring in diverse talent. "When our first financial services person left, I replaced him with a young brother from Detroit." He added, "Again, not from the district but [the member] wanted someone for financial services. I got somebody from financial services; he just happened to be a brother." However, after that hire moved on, he "couldn't find a brother or sister who wanted to come to the Hill for the salary," which ranged between $50,000 and $60,000, so he hired a White woman, and it was just him again as the only Black staffer in the office. However, staffers stay in mid-level roles for three years, on average, which has given him the opportunity to fill this role multiple times.[1]

When the White woman in the financial services role left, Jonathan wanted her replacement to be a person of color. However, "the White woman who left, she tried to go behind my back and try to get somebody else hired," which he shot down. As he described it, the departing staffer recruited "one of their own." If Jonathan were not in his position, business as usual—Whites being in charge and selecting other Whites—would have prevailed, a process that sociologists refer to as White opportunity hoarding.[2] Challenging this self-replicating system takes considerable power. As Jonathan pointed out,

"We don't have people who support us who are calling in and saying 'Hey, we want you to hire this person,'" referencing how he received a phone call recommending one of the White candidates from a US senator and influential lobbyist in their district. He was adamant that the two White finalists he interviewed were "not it." Whereas in the last chapter, we saw how Michelle, another Black staffer, had the power to stop deliberations and make a recommendation based upon her own moral judgment, here we see how Jonathan uses his power to keep a job search open. Both instances demonstrate why racial representation in top staff positions matters for social justice. He eventually hired an Indian American woman for the role, showing his commitment to diverse racial representation beyond hiring Black professionals.

At the time we spoke, he was also in the process of hiring a Latina. This final configuration that allowed him to establish a majority-minority office for the first time, which also brought his DC office to look more like the racial makeup of his district, which was close to being majority-minority itself. He said, "It's not all Black, but it is majority[-minority]." He proclaimed, "I still will tell you that I have the best staff. And again, it's not quantity but it's quality and it just happens to be quantity."

When he could not find suitable candidates of color for policy positions, he recruited people of color for administrative roles. For example, his current staff assistant was a Black man, who greeted me when I visited their office. Lawmakers typically prioritize hiring job candidates from their district for entry-level positions. The "people who sit out front, they know the district and so they're more amenable to tours and people who walk in," he explained. However, for a long time he found it difficult to recruit racially diverse candidates from his district for these roles. He said that in the past, he has called the Congressional Black Caucus Foundation (CBCF) to say, "Send me some interns!" He said those interns are "not working in a CBC office, but they're working for an office and they're working for a Black chief of staff that has an interest in making sure that they excel." This work expands the reach of the Congressional Black Caucus Foundation internship program, which traditionally places Black students in the offices of Black lawmakers. He explained his personal goal was to not only hire Black staffers but to "to create and foster an environment where people can understand what it takes to get to my level," he said. "I make no bones about it; I mean, that's why I'm here." Jonathan is always mentoring diverse talent (by which he can cultivate his own network to recommend others for jobs). In fact, Jonathan had been a mentor for my old chief of staff, a Black woman who had initially connected us.

While Jonathan was willing to go on the record criticizing the lack of racial diversity on Capitol Hill, other senior Black staffers employed a less visible and confrontational strategy. They similarly bragged about having some of the most racially diverse offices on Capitol Hill. However, they downplayed their own active involvement in recruiting diverse talent and instead described the outcomes as naturally occurring. Even still, they called attention to insular hiring practices that primarily benefited White staffers, and they pushed to make hiring more inclusive.

John is one of the first (and few) Black staffers to be a chief of staff in the Senate. As you will remember, he got his job working for a White Republican senator through the assistance of civil rights icon Vernon Jordan in the 1990s. He bragged about having a "high-quality staff." He described the hiring process as many others did: "There were some formal processes up there. You post a job at the job bank. But you know, when we needed a legislative director, when we needed a staffer for a particular portfolio of business, we just asked who's out there." Relying primarily on word of mouth, his staff would refer a stable list of candidates that his legislative director (LD) would then review and make final recommendations. The job candidates would then meet with John and the senator before a final decision would be made.

Although John's staff recruited and screened job candidates, he would intervene if the final candidates all looked the same. "You know, if my LD came back with three White males I'd say, 'Wait a minute, there's no women? There's no Hispanics? There's no African Americans that we could see?' Sometimes I'd say, 'Let's go take another look.'" There are two reasons why John intervened. First, as he plainly put it, "I made a point that we're looking for a diverse group." He argued that it was important for his office to look like the state it represented. "Representing the [state] that had the demographics that it had, it was important in the office to have a staff that was as reflective as possible of that. I think we got close when I was there. It wasn't like we were looking for some particular target. But I think we got close." As he later stated, racial and gender diversity brings with it a "richness of different perspectives" that were invaluable in legislative deliberations. To make his case, he cited a Black woman who worked on his staff and handled health care issues. "She had a perspective that when we weren't thinking about it, she would bring that in. African American, female. And, actually, I will tell you, there were times where—there were issues where the perspective of women on that staff—she would make sure that was injected in. And that was always a good thing."

Echoing Jonathan's sentiment, John emphasized the need to get the best staff. When they were handed a crop of candidates who looked the same, it signaled to him a process that was not competitive but rather guided by convenience. Arguably, having the best staff might mean something different for senior Black staffers who, because of their numerical rarity, experience heightened visibility and greater scrutiny in their leadership roles.[3]

Carla was another senior Black staffer in the Senate. She spoke to me about diversifying her Senate office and what it meant to do this work as a Black woman. She described hiring staff through a mix of direct application and informal methods. "A lot of it was just cold resumes. People would submit a resume, and we would bring them in. We did make a couple of hires this way. A lot was also relationships, which goes back to who you know. We would bring in people who we knew were good people to talk with the senator."

There was a certain tension with how Carla discussed the role of race in the hiring process. She did not think of herself as an "influencer" or a "mover and shaker" on the Hill, even though her high-ranking position made her a powerful figure. Instead, she insisted, "I just come to work, do my best, and go home." Related to hiring, she told me, "I'll interview five people and one is bound to look different—Black, Brown, or whatever. Not that I automatically go to that person. It is not affirmative action. All of our Brown folks are more than qualified." Senior Black staffers like Carla were reluctant to highlight their active role in recruiting and hiring racially diverse talent. Instead, they talked about how they oversaw a fair process where people of color succeeded, underscoring the excellence of these candidates and minimizing their own effort or biases.

Part of the reason why Carla emphasized the qualifications of the staffers of color she hired was because she knew all too well what it felt like to be a Black person in a historically White space. In our interview, she brought up her undergraduate years, attending a majority-White university while affirmative action policies were being litigated at the Supreme Court. As a Black undergraduate, Carla felt like she was on trial herself. "What pissed me off the most is that people thought I did not deserve to be there." Her past experiences influenced how she approached her current job in Congress, another historically White space. "I do not want any of my staff to ever feel that way—that they just got there by their race. So I make sure that everyone is quality." With quality assured, she bragged about having diverse racial representation in every department of her Senate office, including their policy, communication, and administrative teams.

It is hard to ascertain how much effort Carla puts into recruiting and hiring a racially diverse staff because hiring overall in Congress is so opaque. It could be that more people of color apply for positions in her office because it had a reputation for hiring racial minorities, most notably demonstrated by Carla's own presence. This way, Carla's office might attract a more racially diverse applicant pool. It also could be that Carla makes a more concentrated effort to hire professionals from different social backgrounds. The opposite could also be true for other congressional offices, where White staffers control hiring. These offices might also receive fewer applicants of color because Black and Brown candidates might assume that their resume might not be favorably reviewed and that these senior staffers might pay less attention to hiring racially diverse talent. The lack of transparency in congressional hiring makes it difficult to ascertain how Black staffers influence the hiring process. As we've discussed, congressional offices do not disclose demographic information about the job candidates who apply for congressional staff positions. Since congressional hiring is decentralized and determined by individual offices, all of whom have different hiring procedures, it is likely that these data do not even exist.

Improving racial representation among Hill staffers was clearly important to Carla and a problem to which she devoted considerable time, including by mentoring junior staffers of color. Yet she downplayed recruiting staffers of color because she did not want them to be perceived as unqualified. This tension also speaks to the status of senior Black staffers, who want to be respected and trusted and not penalized for their work to even the playing field. "The problem is that we need more people that are willing to allow someone like me to diversify an office, and people are scared to do that. Anyone you bring to the table represents you automatically. I do not think that people want to take that risk." Here, Carla speaks about the reluctance of White Republicans to hire diverse staff and their unwillingness to trust staffers of color to act on their behalf. However, this issue plagues White Democrats as much as it does White Republicans, both of whom fail miserably at hiring and promoting staffers of color. White lawmakers' insecurities and ultimate failures put senior Black staffers like Carla in a tough position. They can either speak openly about a system that privileges Whiteness or minimize the problem at hand as well as their own involvement in fixing it. The problem with the first approach is that it risks further marginalizing staffers of color who speak candidly about how they see their roles and possibly limiting their future success by putting them in a more racialized role, where they focus primarily on racial issues.[4] That is, senators would hire senior Black staffers like Carla if they are interested in diversifying their offices and not for much else. Despite these assumptions that staffers of color who promote more racially inclusive hiring practices are enacting their own agenda, I find that this work is closely associated with advancing lawmakers' interests. As staffers told me, hiring the best staff and having it represent the diversity of their district benefited their lawmaker's policy and political goals.

To Black chiefs of staff, the value that a racially diverse political staff brought to congressional offices was clear.

Melissa told me that racial and gender diversity was at the fore-front of her mind when she approached hiring and the need to create a diverse staff. "Some in the district think her office should be all Black, but we also live in a diverse world, so it's impor-tant to have diversity—Whites, Blacks, Hispanics, you name it. And their backgrounds are important, and their varying levels of exposure are important. It just adds to the value of our office."

Jordan, another Black chief of staff, observed how his White peers struggled to recruit staffers of color and recognize their contributions. "When leadership members hire a diverse staffer, it's usually to handle the diversity issues in your office, and that's usually it. So it's limited on their mindset in terms of what I think diverse staff people can do." He referenced how Democratic lead-ership had made some notable appointments of Black staffers in recent years; however, the pace was slow. He explained that part of this incrementalism was due to anxieties that his White peers had when they hired people of color. "I've been through the process of trying to refer staff to leadership offices and I've seen the anxiety that their chiefs of staff go through in finding the right fit for their office." He shared with me certain concerns that White chiefs of staff may have when considering hiring people of color. "Is he the right person? Will he stay? You know, will he be able to identify? Will he be able to cross over? Will he be able to connect? You know, all of those questions that are important to them that make him cautious about going outside and identify-ing somebody of diverse backgrounds."

Holding Congress Accountable

As Kelly mentioned at the start of this chapter, there are news articles that run, on what seems like an annual publication schedule, that spotlight the lack of racial diversity on the Hill. These articles are typically published in reputable political outlets like *Politico* and *The Hill*, which primarily DC insiders read. The problem is that everyone in the city knows that Capitol Hill is extremely White; consequently, this *news* does not seem newsworthy. That's why in 2006, when *DiversityInc*, a business magazine, ran a story labeling the Senate as the worst employer for diversity, it caused a commotion.[5]

C. Stone Brown and Mark Lowery, the authors, argued that the rate of employment for people of color in the Senate was just not bad; it was among the worst in the country for any major employers. Their investigation found that out of the 4,100 Senate employees across the country, people of color held only 6 percent of these positions. In comparison to the national population and racial representation in the top corporations, their findings are especially noteworthy. At the time, people of color made up 30 percent of the US population and 34 percent of the workforces of the top fifty companies. Additionally, Black professionals held 8.3 and 9.7 percent of management roles nationwide and in the top 50 companies, respectively, compared to 2.9 percent in the Senate.[6]

What's more, the feature article included an enlarged photograph across a two-page spread from the Supreme Court confirmation hearings of Samuel Alito earlier that year. The image was striking and vividly captured the problem at hand. The senators, their staff, and the nominee were all White. This Whiteness would go on unquestioned in the hearing itself, and its implications would last a lifetime.

The story was well received and, as I will explain shortly, had quite an impact. The argument and data were compelling, and the timing was just right. However, reading the article, you might not know former Black Senate staffers originally conceived this idea.

Julian, a former Senate staffer, helped pitch that article and kept a copy of that 2006 issue on his office bookshelf. He handed it to me as we spoke for an hour in his office just off Pennsylvania Avenue. When he started in the Senate in the mid-1990s, he admitted he was so focused on work that he did not realize he was the only person of color in the room. The lack of racial diversity on the Hill did not become apparent to him until he transitioned to the White House. "It struck me that when I went to the White House, there were a lot of us there. This was Clinton's White House and whether it was his Cabinet or the White House staff, it was really diverse. You weren't going to walk around the White House for more than a few minutes before you bumped into somebody." Ironically, Julian's memory of running into so many people of color in the Clinton White House contrasts sharply with Black staffers' view of encountering people of color on Capitol Hill; as we have seen, it feels like a chance encounter for them, especially in the Senate.

Now employed as a lobbyist, Julian formed a working group with other former Black Hill staffers to hold Congress accountable. As he explained, he reached out to the editor of *DiversityInc*, who he had worked with previously in Washington. "So, I basically had him come and sit down with myself and about three or four other people, peers of mine who were in that working group, and we kinda walked him through the problem we saw on the Hill. And focused in on the Senate. And basically—you know, I pitched him that story, even to the point of getting him that *US News & World Report* picture when it came out. And I said, 'You gotta print this picture!'" Julian added that the *DiversityInc* team deserved credit for collecting the data and presenting a compelling narrative, but so did he and his peers—they pitched the idea.

I came across Julian's name multiple times in newspapers as a vocal critic of lawmakers' terrible hiring practices. I asked him about his thoughts on how to fix this persistent problem. Julian offered two strategies. He explained that you can have conversations about what you are missing—i.e., the value of diversity and how it is essential for representative lawmaking. But as he admitted, those conversations can only go so far. This led to his other strategy—shame. "If you want to get a company to move in one direction, well, you know, you can publicly shame them in a way that gets people to move quickly." The tactic worked by providing empirical evidence of the Senate's shady hiring practices to a fresh new audience.

As a result, Senate Majority Leader Harry Reid created the Senate Democratic Diversity Initiative in 2007. "I know that if you talk with people who work for Harry Reid and I worked very closely with his office and leading up to when they decided to create that office, they'll tell you it was this article that caught their attention in a way that made them think— this is no longer sustainable—this is not a good situation, and we got to fix it."

The Senate Democratic Diversity Initiative acts as an interlocutor between Senate offices and job seekers. They work directly with offices to fill vacancies by recommending candidates from their extensive resume bank. They also help train job seekers for the interview process. The Senate Democratic Diversity Initiative has been most successful in altering the racial makeup of staffers in junior- and mid-level positions, which are easier to fill. Another limitation, however, is that senators are not required to work with the initiative at all. Or rather, the office has almost no power to hold senators accountable.

A similar scenario played out almost a decade later. As I mentioned previously, I wrote a policy paper documenting the lack of racial diversity among top senate staffers in 2015. In national and local newspapers, the Joint Center for Political and Economic Studies and I received exclusive credit for this work. However, this report was the idea of the latest cohort of former Black Senate staffers, who were now employed as lobbyists, consultants, and policy and political strategists in the executive branch, nonprofit groups, and corporations. At the beginning of 2015, they met to discuss the persistent underrepresentation of Black professionals in top positions among Senate staffers. They concluded that there needed to be a new empirical report that could once again spur conversation about the lack of racial diversity on the Hill. Those individuals then reached out to the Joint Center with this idea and suggested that I complete this research, given my expertise and research agenda. I had previously interviewed the organizers of this elite group. They orchestrated the publication of the report, connecting me as a researcher to the Joint Center, a reputable think tank focused on Black political issues. What's more, the report would not have been possible without the cooperation of Black staffers currently employed in the Senate, who helped me collect data and verify my findings.

Both of these instances exemplify Black political power. Typically, when we examine Black politics in Washington, the focus is almost exclusively on Black lawmakers, not the Black professionals who work with them on Capitol Hill. Black staffers, of course, do not vote on legislation, but as we have seen in the previous chapter, they help research and write policy as well as provide advice and analysis to their boss. What's more, here we see how they use their expertise and relationships to challenge legislative inequality outside of their formal work responsibilities.

Holding the House of Representatives accountable for its abysmal hiring record is a bit harder. Because of the growing percentage of African American, Latino, and Asian American representatives (who disproportionately hire staffers of color), the House does not appear as bad as the Senate. However, if you peer into the offices of White representatives, you would see that the problem exists on both sides of the Capitol.

Carlos, a Puerto Rican staffer with experience in the House and the Senate, had a natural interest in helping other Latinos get Hill jobs. "I started off just wanting to help people navigate the process. So I'd have coffee with people all the time and meet these very impressive people, and working with the legislature, so we would put them in contact with people in different offices, so that they would know someone and they could help move their resume up. We would review their resumes sometimes for glaring mistakes, we'd let them know about the Hill: these are the positions, this is what to do, if you're interested in this issue, go to briefings, meet these people."

Carlos became frustrated as none of the qualified Latino candidates he recommended got any job offers. "But we kept seeing people not get hired, so it was frustrating. We could often, in this day and age, access resumes of people who did get the positions, and oftentimes, at least on paper, they were less qualified. Now I don't want to say in any individual case, they may have been wonderful, I'm just looking at a sheet of paper that I find online about who they are, and oftentimes, our people were more qualified." To this end, Carlos took a more confrontational approach to address racist hiring practices; he worked with the Congressional Hispanic Staff Association to publish *Unrepresented*, a report documenting the absence of Latinos in top staff positions on the Hill.[7]

The 2010 report found that, in the Senate, "there is currently only one Latino chief of staff, though if taken as a proportion of the US Latino population, there would be fifteen. In addition, there is not a single Latino legislative director in the Senate and only one staff director out of the forty top committee positions." The House did not fare much better: "Latinos made up only 2.7 percent of chiefs of staff and 2.1 percent of legislative directors." Again, these are the most influential staff roles, and it is utterly shameful that the largest racial minority group is so inadequately represented on Capitol Hill.

Confronting lawmakers takes courage. Carlos described how even though the report was well received, many were scared to hold Congress accountable because the confrontational strategy could backfire. "We met with the Hispanic Lobbyists Association, we met with the National Hispanic Leadership Agenda, they were supportive, but it's not their main issue." As he pointed out, many big advocacy groups don't want to openly criticize Congress for fear of how it might affect their working relationships with lawmakers. Referring to some of the large Latino advocacy groups, he explained, "They're trying to work with members to pass immigration reform, so they're very worried to pick this up as an issue, which is part of the problem—no one wants to criticize." Going public has its costs, especially for staffers themselves. "Even as staff, we don't want to be blasting Pelosi. I'm a Democrat. We'll criticize her, but it's very muted and it's careful. As a staffer, you're not supposed to be the one on the front page." Carlos's candid comments underscore the risk that congressional staffers take when they criticize lawmakers. Their jobs are on the line. However, it also says a lot when staffers are willing to break the norms of staffers being invisible and go public with their frustrations of racial problems that seemingly won't go away.

At the same time, the critique that Carlos levied against Latino lawmakers equally applies to Black lawmakers (and Black advocacy groups too). Black staff confided, often with requests to be off the record, that Black lawmakers weren't doing enough to challenge White lawmakers' racist hiring practices. Presumably, in the House, where Black lawmakers' power is the greatest, you would expect, at least when Democrats control the chamber, that legislative inequality would be at the forefront of the House agenda, but it is not. The reluctance of the Black caucus to foreground racial equity in their own House as an important policy issue is an indication of how the contemporary cohort of Black lawmakers is much more moderate than their forebearers, whose radicalism often put them at odds with members of their own party. Consequently, Black staffers have stepped up where Black lawmakers have stepped back.

Going on the Record

For over an hour, Carla, a top Black staffer in the Senate, spoke to me about her career, balancing motherhood, managing staff across several offices, guiding her senator, and the merits of diversity. She spoke in hushed tones, holding the microphone meant for her lapel tight in her hands and close to her lips. As she discussed systemic racism, she surveyed the almost empty cafeteria in the basement of the Russell Senate Office Building and monitored the proximity of potential eavesdroppers. She was one the highest-ranking women of color in the Senate, and while our conversation was confidential, what she said could easily be taken out of context and reported. I emailed her the day prior after receiving her contact information from another staffer. She promptly responded and asked if we could meet the following week after the Senate adjourned for its Fourth of July weeklong break. I was not available to meet then, but fortunately she told me she had an opening the following afternoon. I was surprised that as one of the top staffers in her Senate office, she had a free hour the day before Congress recessed, which is a frantic period filled with last-minute votes and schedules that are typically not your own. However, what was most revealing was simply that she decided to spend this time with me.

For over five years, I had the privilege of interviewing these elite political professionals about intimate aspects of their professional lives. Some of these participants had high-ranking positions and had worked in various presidential administrations, and occupied senior roles in lobbying, consulting, and nonprofit organizations, not to mention top positions in Congress. I was often surprised when many of these individuals responded to my requests and agreed to speak with me. I was even more taken aback when they spent hours during their workdays to answer my questions and provided in-depth accounts of their experiences in the political world. Their desire to speak candidly and at length was undoubtedly influenced by their seeing a problem. The racial inequality that I inquired about was never news to them. However, they often saw me as a person who could finally expose what they had known for years. Their generosity is also an impressive display of their own power to use me to fulfill their aims of unmasking Congress as a racialized institution.

In this chapter, I examined how Black staffers challenge insular hiring practices that perpetuate the congressional workplace as an inequality regime. Among the senior Black staffers I interviewed, all of them recognized the need to have racially diverse offices. Additionally, in our conversations, they highlighted that their offices represented the nation's diversity. For some, like Jonathan, this meant an exhaustive search to find diverse talent, establishing a high bar for excellence along the way. Others, like Carla, said that their diverse teams were naturally occurring. Black staffers also held lawmakers accountable for who they hire by working behind the scenes to make legislative inequality a public story. This strategy was risky but effective because it illuminated the opaqueness of the congressional workplace with empirical evidence. Similar to what we learned in the previous chapter, this work, which combines individual and collective efforts, exists on a continuum, with some Black staffers being more active and engaged than others in efforts to confront White domination on Capitol Hill.

CHAPTER SIX

What Congress
Should Look Like

CAPITOL HILL LOOKS different these days. I conducted my last interview in 2015, a moment in Congress that seems almost impossibly quaint compared to today's rancor and dysfunction. But while Congress is frequently villainized for all that is wrong in politics today, we can also make the opposite argument: Congress is offering us a glimpse of what is possible, both today and in the years to come, in American politics.

Congress is home to a new and growing cohort of men and women of color. Their stories are many, and inspiring. In 2018, Ayanna Pressley defeated a ten-term White Democratic representative to become the first Black woman elected to Congress from Massachusetts. During her campaign, Pressley argued that she would bring "activist-leadership" to Congress and stumped that "the people closest to the pain should be closest to the power." She also persuasively argued that constituents of the state's only majority-minority district deserved leadership that looked like them.[1] At the same time that Black candidates are winning in majority-minority districts, they are also winning in districts that are majority-White. That same year, Lauren Underwood made history as the youngest Black woman ever elected to Congress. A former nurse, she successfully campaigned on improving health care access and affordability. She resoundingly defeated six White men in her Democratic primary and then ousted the four-term White Republican incumbent in an Illinois district that is 85 percent White.[2] Pressley and Underwood are a part of a new class of progressive talent who ascended to power to challenge the racist, sexist, xenophobic policies of former President Donald Trump and his Republican allies.

In 2020, Mondaire Jones and Ritchie Torres became the first openly gay Black men elected to the House of Representatives. They campaigned to be champions for the nation's poor and vowed to strengthen our democracy for everyone. All of these Black members have risen to popularity by asserting bold progressive ideas and defeating White lawmakers. This new generation of Black leaders also includes members like Cori Bush, who are challenging moderate Black lawmakers, arguing that this old guard does not understand the urgency of the moment and are not doing enough to help poor Black voters. These new Black members are joined by other lawmakers of color, like Representatives Sharice Davids and Mary Peltola, who are Indigenous American; Representative Alexandria Ocasio-Cortez and Senator Catherine Cortez Masto, who are Puerto Rican and Mexican, respectively; and Representatives Andy Kim, Ami Bera, Rashida Tlaib, who are Korean American, Indian American, and Palestinian American, respectively.

It is now common to read headlines at the beginning of each new Congress that read, "The most diverse congress ever." In the 118th Congress (2023–24), 151 lawmakers identified as Black, Hispanic, Asian/Pacific Islander, or Native American.

This includes sixty-three Black Americans, sixty-two Latino Americans, twenty-one Asian Americans, and five Native Americans. Collectively, a quarter of all voting members of Congress are people of color.[3] Most of this racial and ethnic diversity is in the House and among Democrats. In this latest session, only eleven senators identify as Black, Latino, or Asian. This trend toward greater racial representation among lawmakers is promising, albeit a far cry from truly reflecting the country's diversity. White men and women continue to be disproportionately represented among members of Congress. Non-Hispanic Whites account for 75 percent of voting members, even while they make up just 59 percent of the national population.[4] Increasing racial and gender representation is essential for improving the image of Congress. While the legislature is still a White space, these new diverse faces show how Capitol Hill can also be a space to achieve racial justice.

Greater racial representation among lawmakers has led to greater attention on Congress. In 2019, Michael Cohen, President Trump's former attorney, testified before the House Committee on Oversight and Reform. He admitted that the president was a racist, a conman, and a cheat.[5] His admissions were newsworthy, but what stood out from that hearing was the intense questioning he faced from newly sworn-in Representatives Ocasio-Cortez, Tlaib, and Pressley. An image of the three women staring down the Trump defector went viral. They meant business, and this image helped show how Democrats would stand up to the lawlessness of the Trump administration. Social media users instantly made the image a meme, inserting their own captions for what can only be described as a purely bad-ass moment.

Congressional hearings are highly scripted events, of course, that focus on finding facts and making news. It is one of the rare opportunities that the public has to view Congress actually working. However, while hearings are an important aspect of how Congress conducts its business, these televised events distort how the institution works. Congressional hearings reinforce a false narrative about how Congress works by foregrounding lawmakers and rendering staffers invisible. Legislative staffers, as we have seen, are the individuals who have organized these hearings, found witnesses, drafted questions, and written remarks. In hearings, some staffers are seated behind lawmakers while others view the proceedings from their offices. From either location, the work of these political staffers is unknown and ignored.

Representative Pressley commented on the viral photo by tweeting an expanded version of the photograph that included several staffers seated behind her. She told her followers to get a "glimpse of some of the women behind this woman." She elaborated, "Grateful to my dedicated A team and the committee staff for this diligent preparation that went into yesterday's hearing."[6] While many lawmakers claim exclusive credit for their work, Pressley acknowledged how her success was facilitated by her staff. This admission might be because Pressley was once a congressional staffer herself. She began her political career working for Senator Ted Kennedy. Throughout her congressional career, Pressley has highlighted the work of congressional staff, elevating in particular the unique contributions of staffers of color. During Black History Month in February 2020, Pressley used her personal Twitter account to celebrate a different Black staffer each day.[7] These acknowledgements matter, especially when Black staffers continue to be underrepresented in top staff positions.

The congressional workforce is diversifying at a much slower pace than members of Congress. Between 2018 and 2022 the percentage of people of color in top staff positions in the House has only modestly increased, from 13.7 percent to

18 percent. Specifically, despite comprising 12 and 18 percent of the national population, respectively, Blacks and Latinos together account for only 5.6 percent and 5.8 percent of the top House staffers. The Senate is much worse. Between 2015 and 2020, the percentage of people of color in top staff positions grew from 7 percent to 11 percent. Accordingly, Blacks and Latinos hold 3.1 and 3.8 percent of top staff positions in senators' personal offices. Finally, racial representation in congressional committees, where a lot lawmaking occurs, is also alarmingly low. In the House and the Senate, people of color only represent 17.1 percent and 7.9 percent of staff directors, respectively.

As we have learned, it matters who holds these positions of power. It affects the laws that are made and who ascends to greater positions of power in politics, all of which shape our lived realities. Accordingly, in the pages that remain, I will describe how we can make the congressional workplace more representative of the national population. To achieve this goal, we must radically change and end how Congress operates as an inequality regime, shedding its opaque veneer. I see this work to make the congressional workplace more inclusive and equal as connected to broader reforms to modernize Congress and strengthen its capacity to lead as the first branch of government.

Transforming Congress

The designation of Congress as the last plantation is an effective rhetorical strategy that demonstrates how the institution has evaded its own racial reckoning. It is a denunciation and diagnosis all at once. Black women and men use the plantation as shorthand to describe a place of racism, whether of a bygone era in the slave-saturated South, or a more enduring, albeit less obvious, contemporary manifestation. It is code for an organization made up by a racial hierarchy and one that dispenses unfair treatment to Black and Brown folks. The designation immediately crystallizes the problem at hand on Capitol Hill. At the same time, this scandalous classification obscures how Congress is a different type of racialized institution. While Congress might look like other White-dominated institutions, the reasons for this are quite different from what make other organizations White. And for that reason, the path toward progress is different. As we have seen, the congressional workplace is reminiscent of a spoils system, where lawmakers have free rein to manage their offices, and the rules are either nonexistent, confusing, or easily ignored. What's more, this structure, shaped by racial, gender, and, class processes, is opaque and avoids external scrutiny and accountability. To this end, reforming Congress must mean making the congressional workplace a more transparent, accountable, and accessible institution.

Congress must be subject to the same demographic reporting requirements that lawmakers themselves have mandated for private employers in federal law. These data would provide a detailed understanding of racial disparities among congressional staff, not just about who is hired, but who is promoted and who is terminated. This kind of data—clear and compelling and simple to understand—reveals disparities that are then much harder to ignore. In other settings, these data subject White-dominated organizations to immense criticism and protest. But this external pressure, instrumental in making White organizations change, is missing from Capitol Hill. It is hard to hold lawmakers accountable when our understanding of the problem is incomplete. Relatedly, these rules should also apply to the White House and the Supreme Court, both of which do not publish any demographic information on their employees. Ironically, the Supreme Court has been referred to as the "Second to Last Plantation."[8]

I believe that this kind of data transparency is the single most important way to prompt congressional accountability, and I have seen the change that can happen as a result. As discussed earlier, I wrote a policy paper in 2015 that documented how staffers of color held only 7 percent of top positions in the Senate. The report, published by the Joint Center for Economic and Political Studies, gained immediate attention in the news media. This empirical data mobilized grassroots activists, who then pressured Senate Democrats to hire more staffers of color and to release more transparent hiring data. As a result, since 2017, Senate Democrats have released racial demographic data for their personnel and committee offices annually. To be sure, these data are not perfect. Senate Democrats provide aggregate level data only, which include, roughly, the staffers employed both in DC and state offices. These aggregate data are an easy way to inflate the number of staffers of color. Lawmakers are more likely to hire staffers of color to work in their state offices; these staffers will engage in public-facing constituent service work rather than the more high-profile policy work that happens almost exclusively in DC.[9] Additionally, these data cannot tell us if staffers of color are equally represented across positions or concentrated in the lower rungs of the office hierarchy, like as receptionists or office administrators, positions that offer lower pay and limited influence in policymaking. Nonetheless, these data, while limited, start to illustrate a picture of who works in congressional offices and, in turn, start to offer a method to hold elected officials accountable. For example, 2020 data showed that the racial compositions of the staff of the two California senators—Dianne Feinstein and Kamala Harris—were drastically different. In Senator Feinstein's office, 32 percent of staff identified as non-White, compared to 61 percent of staff in Senator Harris's office. The gap is noteworthy considering both Democrats represented the same state, where 60 percent of residents identify as either Latino, Asian, or African American. Congress needs to expand upon the work of Senate Democrats to collect and publish more transparent employment data.

In 2021, I testified before the House Committee on the Modernization of Congress on how to make congressional internships more accessible to students of color. My main recommendation was for the House to collect demographic information on interns as an equity measure to identify if their new program, which allocated funding to congressional offices to pay interns, did so equitably. This committee, which investigated and evaluated a wide range of proposals to modernize Congress, made it one of its recommendations to collect demographic data on employees through an optional form at employee onboarding. Consequently, the Office of the Chief Administrative Officer in the House, the agency created to oversee its day-to-day operations, is scheduled to begin collecting this data in the 118th Congress (2023–24). This is an extraordinary feat, which will allow researchers as well as the House on its own to better know the House workforce. Unfortunately, the Senate, which manages its workforce separately, has yet to take any meaningful action on this front. We must force senators to do the same. Adhering to demographic reporting requirements mandated for large employers is but one step of a larger process required to professionalize the congressional workplace.

It is common among lawmakers, staffers, and even political scientists to compare congressional offices to small businesses. The metaphor is well intentioned and is meant to explain how the idiosyncratic personalities of lawmakers create wide variation in the operation and management of House and Senate offices.

However, this small business mentality has unintended consequences. It fosters an ethos where anything goes. This mentality allows lawmakers and their top aides to sidestep rules and ignore the rights and needs of workers at the bottom of the legislative hierarchy. It invites corruption, exploitation, and inequality into the Capitol. We must think about congressional offices as what they are, government offices supported by taxpayers, not small businesses. Lawmakers will always be in charge of their offices; however, the current system is too decentralized and allows for wide variation in how offices are run. This is evident in how prospective Hill staffers must navigate through the uncertainty of insular hiring practices to find congressional employment. It's time to prioritize good employment practices in Congress. Lawmakers should look at the federal civil service as an appropriate model for how to achieve these goals. For example, there are clear points of entry into the federal bureaucracy along with well-defined criteria for hiring and promotion.

House Democrats, during the 116th Congress, took a big step in confronting legislative inequality by creating the House Office for Diversity and Inclusion. The office, which is independent and nonpartisan, acts as a broker between House offices and job seekers. The office provides resume reviews for job seekers and, working with staff associations, recommends promising job candidates to House offices. What's more, the office is also playing a larger role in making the House more inclusive and equitable. It has already issued reports analyzing compensation, benefits, demographics, and even witness diversity on committees. However, the office is also limited. Its effectiveness depends on members and offices listening to it and following its recommendations. What's more, House Republicans have continually sought to defund the office now that they have a majority in the chamber.

Finally, we must make Congress a better place to work. The congressional workplace features high turnover among staffers, effectively making congressional offices a steppingstone rather than a destination. Staffers hustle for a few short years, underpaid and overworked, learning the ins and outs of lawmaking and the who's who of politics, only to cash out working for corporations and lobbying firms. This makes the real winners in this situation elite industries, which use their new hires to gain the upper hand in policymaking conversations to obtain favorable outcomes that reward their bottom line. Members should stop subsidizing the training and recruitment of employment for billion-dollar corporations and instead reward and retain their own workers.[10]

In their policy report, *Congressional Brain Drain*, political scientists Alexander Furnas and Tim LaPira analyzed survey data from eight hundred staffers about their career plans. Their findings are noteworthy. Sixty-five percent of the staffers planned to leave Congress within five years, and only a handful, 6 percent, anticipated working on the Hill until they retired. It is a massive loss to Congress that it can expect to lose more than half of its workforce in five years. While roughly half intended to stay in government, 43 percent planned to move to the private sector. Furnas and LaPira concluded, "For the most part, working on the Hill is an entry-level position for K Street, rather than a stepping stone for a career in public service."

Next to the White House, Congress stands as the second most influential political workplace in the country. Getting a job in the White House is even more difficult than Congress, owing to its stature and limited number of positions. However, if you can get a job in Congress, perhaps by knowing the right people, or through persistence and grit applying over and over again, then it can be a powerful opportunity that educates you about the policymaking process and credentials you to work in higher levels of politics. As many staffers told me, congressional employment is often a prerequisite for high-level political jobs, and you are best positioned to get this necessary experience in during your twenties and early thirties, when you have more energy and time to commit to long hours and before you have more financial responsibilities that prevent you from taking a low-paying job. After you do your time on the Hill, you have greater opportunities to work in other political workplaces, whether it is the White House or lobbying. But you have to go through Congress first. However, the exclusionary nature of Congress, including its insular recruitment and hiring practices as well as its pay structure, creates an unequal base that is then amplified throughout Washington and the rest of the country.

The most compelling possibility for retaining its workers is the most obvious one: Congress should pay their workers more. Lawmakers earn $174,000 per annum while some of the lowest-paid staff must work second jobs as Uber drivers and bartenders just to get by. Lawmakers are finally starting to pay attention to staff salaries, which media outlets have covered with increasing fervor in recent years. In her last two years as Speaker of the House, Nancy Pelosi twice raised the maximum amount staffers can earn, bringing this sum to $212,000. To be sure, this is a lot of money. But top staffers who leave Capitol Hill can expect to earn as much and more in the private sector. At the same, the decision to raise the salary cap for top staffers, who, as we have learned, are overwhelmingly White, drew considerable ire from staffers, the vast amount of whom do not earn anything near that high sum. As a result, Pelosi established a $45,000 minimum for House staff. Historically, federal lawmakers have resisted spending large sums on staff salaries as a practice of good financial stewardship of taxpayer dollars.[11] But this perspective is shortsighted. A well-staffed congressional workforce is the backbone of a functioning and effective legislative branch. Congressional staff salaries are below what similar professionals in the executive branch and private industries earn. This disparity is disgraceful and exclusionary. Meager salaries are policy decisions that all but guarantee that only the affluent can participate in lawmaking. It literally forces those who are less affluent to work twice as hard to be in Congress. What's more, because men of color and women of all backgrounds are more likely to occupy low-paid junior staff positions, this policy decision to pay staff so little is inherently racist and sexist. It also creates a foundation for a racially stratified political system.

Congressional staff have almost no bargaining power over their salaries, benefits, or working conditions. However, in almost all other work settings, employees can unionize to advocate for themselves. The House authorized its staffers to unionize in 2022, but the Senate has yet to act. Lawmakers can increase salaries and expand benefits for workers, but without the right to unionize, congressional workers are still subject to the whims of their omnipotent bosses. And as congressional history demonstrates, this means the rights of Capitol Hill workers are in jeopardy, as is their dignity.

There is a growing chorus of lawmakers who see the need for a racially and economically diverse congressional workforce and recognize that the only way to attract and retain this talent is to offer better compensation and benefits. They, too, understand that legislative inequality undermines the credibility of Congress as a democratic institution and undercuts their own abilities to fulfill their constitutional duties as leaders of the first branch of government. These were the major findings of the House Committee on the Modernization of Congress.

In modernizing the congressional workplace, lawmakers have the opportunity to model what an equitable, fair, and just twenty-first century workplace should be. This would position the legislature as the *first branch* of government, one that leads and does not evade its responsibilities. Leaving behind the metaphor of the "last plantation." Lawmakers like Senators John Glenn, John Heinz, and John McCain used the plantation metaphor to highlight legislative hypocrisy.[12] To extinguish Congress's racist and exclusionary past, lawmakers can begin a new era where they lead by example. They could provide congressional workers with competitive salaries, affordable and comprehensive health care, access to low-cost childcare, flexible work schedules for caregivers, well-paid internships and fellowships, safe and healthy work standards, and the right to unionize. These benefits should extend further: to the vast army of congressional workers that propel congressional operations like carpenters, cooks, and custodians; clerks and stenographers; and police officers and librarians. This would be a remarkable example of congressional leadership beyond what lawmakers can achieve through lawmaking and one that has far-reaching effects for our democracy. That Congress has at least started some of this work is promising, but it will require the participation of all us to see this vision enacted.

How We Make Congress Look Different

Oscar De Priest, the first African American elected to Congress after Reconstruction, eloquently underscored the imperative of confronting racism within the very heart of the legislature: "If we allow segregation and the denial of constitutional rights under the Dome of the Capitol, where in God's name will we get them?"[13] As he testified, legislative inequality is an important public issue that stymies our democracy and perpetuates White supremacy, but it is a problem that does not receive a lot of attention. Making Congress more inclusive and representative requires all of us: ordinary citizens, lawmakers, scholars, popular social movements, and democracy reform groups. We must collectively take up the cause to realize a more inclusive and equitable Congress. To do this, we must expand our understanding of who are the key actors involved in the creation, maintenance, and reproduction of racial domination. We must include behind-the-scenes actors, like congressional staff, as a part of the powerful people who help shape the nation's racial politics. Philosopher Charles Mills provocatively characterized White supremacy as a political system, drawing attention to how racism requires an organizational structure to be enacted.[14] Our political system manifests as a series of complex workplaces that are organized around exclusionary principles and where Whiteness has been the main criterion for admission. The exclusion of people of color from positions within these workplaces, especially senior roles, represents a unique form of marginalization through which they are excluded from making the racial policy that is then imposed on them, as well as on the nation as a whole.

What's more, these jobs often lead staffers to become elected officials themselves. For example, in the 116th Congress (2018–20) a fifth of lawmakers previously worked as staffers or interns, which demonstrates that before you can lead on Capitol Hill you need to work there. Congressional work experience has given leading political figures a mirror to assess their own talents and how they could be of service to the nation. Before Kamala Harris became the highest-ranking woman elected in American government, she began her political career as an intern for California Senator Alan Cranston (a position she would later occupy before becoming vice president). This is the power of working in Congress—it grooms individuals to take the reins of power. These jobs, in other words, show how power is cultivated in American politics, and how it can be more widely distributed.

To meet these democratic goals, we should apply the same public pressure and grassroots infrastructure to diversifying the individuals who hold staff positions that we do for electing men of color and women of all backgrounds to office. We should normalize asking questions to political candidates about who they employ and following up to see if people of color are equally represented across staff positions, or if these leaders only hire racial minorities to handle racial issues and as ambassadors from their office to these same communities. An all-White political staff should serve as grounds for disqualification for any candidate or current office holder aspiring to lead our diverse and multiracial democracy. When we examine a candidate's policy positions, we should examine how they treat the people closest to them—their workers—to see how they will advocate for individuals they do not know. An antiracist future for our nation is not possible if all the decision-makers and political professionals who support them are White.

Scholarly research can play a large role in amplifying legislative inequality in public discourse. To this end, how we study Congress matters. For too long, race-neutral perspectives, which privilege Whiteness and ignore the presence of sweeping inequality, have dominated congressional studies. Centering historically excluded groups in political analysis can illuminate new dimensions of a well-studied institution and further reveal the exact contours of legislative power. In this way, we must build on the already impressive body of research in the fields of racial and ethnic politics. Future research should investigate the experiences of Latinos, Asian Americans, and Native American workers in the Capitol as well as intersecting forces like gender, class, sexuality, and disability among these groups. Moreover, there is a need to go beyond the experiences of professional staff who work in personal, committee, and leadership offices. We know very little about the careers of non-partisan staff, service workers, and Capitol police officers. We should apply a peopled perspective to the study of Congress.[15] Sociologists can and should play a big role in this effort. Sociology has a variety of disciplinary theories, methods, and questions that can improve the public understanding of Congress and its relationship to power and inequality.

Within Congress itself, the Congressional Black Caucus, Congressional Hispanic Caucus, and Congressional Asian Pacific American Caucus (collectively known as the Tri-Caucus) as well as progressive lawmakers should prioritize combating legislative inequality as a part of their social justice agenda.[16] During a period of widespread racial reckoning, lawmakers must resist the urge to exclusively look outward as the only way to respond to urgent calls to address systemic racism. If Congress is to have an important role in helping us achieve an antiracist future, they can only do so if they first clean up their own house (which, presumably, is where their power is the greatest).

Finally, we should consider addressing legislative inequality as an exciting opportunity to realize the democratic promise of Congress as the *People's House*. Opening the doors to the Capitol would admit historically excluded groups and establish increasingly diverse political staffs. Inclusive hiring practices can offer diverse staffs that are better equipped at problem solving and developing innovative public policy solutions.[17] What's more, all of this could help strengthen congressional capacity and rebuild the public image of Congress, which has long been marred by low public approval ratings.

These days, there is a lot on lawmakers' plates. Whether it is regulating A.I. and social media, confronting climate change, building a social infrastructure to support caregivers, or the perennial issue of the economy, there is much to do. On many of the pressing issues facing our country, Congress simply is not leading. Instead, public policy is increasingly being shaped by the executive branch, either through the issuance of executive orders by the president or through rulemaking by departments and agencies. Furthermore, the courts are playing an increasingly significant role in determining public policy. Lawmaking is the job of Congress; but this work is being completed by other branches of government. Congress, the first branch of government mentioned in the US Constitution and the one that is discussed the most, is supposed to have a leading role creating the rules that shape our everyday lives because it is the branch of our federal government that is closest to the people. Partisanship, for sure, explains some of the lawmakers' abdication of leadership on important policy matters. Another important factor is that Congress simply does not have the capacity, both in terms of size of the congressional workforce and expertise within it, to do this work.[18]

Between 1979 and 2021, the number of House staff grew from 8,831 to 9,034, or 2.3 percent. Additionally, in the Senate, from 1987 to 2020, the number of all staff grew from 4,916 to 5,723, or 16.42 percent.[19] Since the 1980s, the US population has grown by more than 100 million, and our economy and society have become advanced, all of which increase the responsibilities of Congress. Staff-level trends show that representatives and senators have not invested in staff, which is a key resource they need to be effective governing leaders.

At the same time, lawmakers are underinvesting in their staff, and we know that its workforce is far from representative. This creates a double threat for our multiracial democracy. We can fix both of these problems together, which can be an exciting opportunity to build a stronger and more representative Congress. But we must foreground inclusive and equitable principles to guide us in this endeavor.

The Afterlife of the Last Plantation

There is a certain irony—and perhaps a certain danger—in suggesting that Congress's "plantation" is the last one, and thus, implicitly, the only one. As we know, this is patently false: there are many plantations still standing today. Some have become tourist attractions or, regrettably, wedding venues; others have become museums and monuments where visitors can learn about our racist past. And then, there are plantations that have been built upon and repurposed. On these stained grounds, the past and the present collide to imagine a more hopeful and just future.

After the Civil War, federal and state governments, churches, and philanthropists supported the formation of colleges and universities to educate African Americans. Many of these institutions, dedicated to educating nearly four million formerly enslaved laborers, were built on the land of former plantations. For example, Hampton University, chartered in 1868, was built on a 160-acre "Wood Farm." The university describes the main building as a "southern colonial style mansion house" built before 1867. Hampton University's most famous graduate, Booker T. Washington, led Tuskegee University, another Black college, from its establishment in 1881 to 1915. Originally, Washington, the sole teacher, ran the school from a one-room shanty. However, under his eminent leadership the school quickly relocated to a hundred-acre abandoned plantation nearby. Washington, himself born into slavery, viewed education as essential for the progress of African Americans and the way that they could establish a life of self-sufficiency. He facilitated the acquisition of the plantation for $500. He converted a hen-house and stable into recitation rooms and led students, after their daily lessons, in clearing the fields and planting their first crops. The irony here is clear.

Almost two decades earlier, enslaved Black men and women who lived on this plantation could not have received an education, and they labored for their enslavers, not themselves. This history points to the complicated legacy of plantations—they are sites of racial domination but also inextricably bound to Black modernity.[20]

On sites of slavery, African Americans envisioned and worked toward achieving a radically different future for themselves as a free people and as engaged citizens. Literary scholar Jarvis McInnis defines this as reterritorialization: "The process by which African Americans attempt to reconcile and imagine a new relationship to land, agriculture, and the earth, outside of and directly opposed to the exploitative racial capitalist regimes engendered by the plantation, sharecropping, and debt peonage." However, the fact that many plantations were reterritorialized as educational institutions points to how African Americans, nearly from the moment slavery was abolished, were building and accumulating Black capital—the skills, values, and relationships necessary for personal and collective progress. The history and afterlives of plantations are instructive for contemplating the future of Congress and the status of African Americans within it.[21]

Every time I walk through the Capitol I am flooded with a mix of emotions. I feel the weight of Whiteness, communicated by an endless sea of White bodies in the halls and White portraiture on the walls, and a certain chilliness that distinctly signals to people who look like me that we do not belong here. Those feelings change when I see another Black man or woman. It could be a staffer, one of the older Black women who works in the cafeteria, or a Black service man dressed in his powder blue uniform. When I see them, I feel like I am at home. We almost always acknowledge each other, either through sustained eye contact or perhaps through a subtle nod. We may not know one another, but there is a connection and the sense of community. The presence of this community of Black men and women is subversive and a reminder that within this elite White space there is an active attempt to reterritorialize the Capitol to serve the interests of African Americans and other marginalized groups who have been historically excluded.

NOTES

Introduction

1. (L. Brown 1989)

2. I am part of a distinguished lineage of Black sociologists that traces its origins back to W.E.B. Du Bois (Hunter 2018). Within this lineage, there is a strong emphasis on capitalizing the term "Black" (Grundy 2022; Shedd 2015). As Du Bois himself famously stated, "I believe that eight million Americans are entitled to a capital letter" (Du Bois and Eaton 1899, 1). Whereas I capitalize Black to recognize and celebrate Black people and culture, I capitalize "White" to interrogate the invisibility of Whiteness.

3. (Chetty et al. 2019; Derenoncourt et al. 2022; Oliver and Shapiro 2013)

4. In *Documenting Desegregation*, sociologists Kevin Stainback and Donald Tomaskovic-Devey (2012) investigated the effects of the Civil Rights Act on the career experiences of Black men, Black women, and White women relative to White men. They found that from the passage of this law until 1980, Black men and Black women made tremendous gains in the workplace, and White women had uninterrupted success until approximately 2000.

5. New research has demonstrated the limited gains achieved from antidiscrimination legislation. For example, Edelman (2016, 1992) indicates how organizations respond to ambiguous antidiscrimination law by creating a variety of policies and programs designed to symbolize attention to the law. She argues that the meaning of law evolves through the articulation and resolutions of problems not in governing institutions such as Congress but rather in the halls of work organizations. As a result, this endogenous process yields limited gain for women and racial minorities.

6. For example, lawmakers have also exempted the legislative branch from the Freedom of Information Act and whistleblower protections.

7. (North 1978)

8. Handling of Discrimination Complaints in the Senate: Hearing before the Committee on Governmental Affairs, US Senate, 95th Congress, 2nd Session, February 9, 1978, Part 2, 10.

9. (United States Congress, House Committee on House Administration, and United States Congress, House Office of History and Preservation, 2008)

10. (Ray 2019; Wooten 2019; Wooten and Couloute 2017; Nkomo 1992)

11. (Carter 2003; Smith 2005)

12. (Bourdieu 1984; Nelson 2016)

13. (Hill Collins 2009)

14. (Omi and Winant 2015)

15. Hiram Revels was the first African American to serve in Congress. He served in the Senate from 1870 to 1871. Joseph H. Rainey is the first African American to serve in the US House of Representatives and the longest-serving Black lawmaker during Reconstruction (1870–1879).

16. While there is limited historical information about African Americans who worked in the Capitol during the early nineteenth century, one example is Tobias Simpson, who worked as a Senate messenger. He helped save the Senate records when the British invaded and burned the Capitol in 1814. Without the valiant efforts of Simpson and Senate Clerk Lewis Manchen, the executive records of the first twenty-five years of the Senate would be lost. Additionally, Kate Masur (2010) documents how members of Congress first hired Black workers in large numbers during Reconstruction.

17. Alice Dunnigan was one of the first African American reporters to be credentialed in Congress. In a four-part series, she highlighted Black workers in the Capitol, including many who had been employed for decades (Dunnigan 1950, 1949b, 1949a).

18. (Rosenthal 2000, 41)

19. (Jones 2019)

20. (Ritchie and You 2019; Dittmar 2021)

21. (Hill Collins 2009; Hunter and Robinson 2018; Young 2004)

22. (P. H. Collins 1993)

23. (Acker 2006, 443)

24. (Dittmar 2021; Carnes 2013; Rosenthal and Bell 2003; Rosenthal 2002; Ritchie and You 2019)

25. (Ray 2019; Watkins-Hayes 2009; Wingfield 2019, 2013; Moore 2008)

26. Here I draw upon Sewell's (1992) idea of structural duality, which explains how organizational structures constrain human behavior but also how individuals have agency to change these same structures. Applied to Congress, this concept demonstrates how Congress is more malleable than we think. I am also inspired by Alondra Nelson's (2016) work analyzing how racialized institutions reckon with their racist pasts, which she terms institutional morality.

27. (King and Smith 2005)

28. More than 1,800 members of Congress enslaved Black men and women; comparatively, 187 African Americans have served in Congress (Weil, Blanco, and Dominguez 2022; Office of the Historian 2023).

29. Richard Russell represented Georgia for nearly forty years in the US Senate, from 1933 to 1971. During his tenure, he authored legislation to remove Blacks from the South and blocked, for decades, any attempt to protect Black civil rights (Mann 2007).

30. (Romzek 2000; Romzek and Utter 1997; Fox and Hammond 1977; Kofmehl 1977; Montgomery and Nyhan 2017; Burgat 2020)

31. (Malbin 1980)

32. (Bartels 2009)

33. (Deering and Smith 1997)

34. (Omi and Winant 2015; Bracey 2015; Bonilla-Silva 1997)

35. (Charles W. Mills 1997; Murakawa 2014; Bateman, Katznelson, and Lapinski 2018; Katznelson 2005; Johnson 2016; Lieberman 2001; Gowayed 2022)

36. (Brenson 2022, 2020)

37. (Tomaskovic-Devey and Avent-Holt 2019)

38. (Torres-Spelliscy 2017)

39. (Montgomery and Nyhan 2017)

40. For example, Traister (2022) writes about the diminished capacity of Senator Dianne Feinstein, who has experienced serious health issues at her advanced age and heavily relies on her staff.

41. (McCrain 2018; Cain and Drutman 2014)

42. (C. Wright Mills 2000)

43. David Mayhew (1974) describes on the first page of his classic book, *Congress: The Electoral Connection*, how political scientists in the 1950s and 1960s borrowed heavily from sociology to study Congress. In addition, Richard Fenno's important work across many decades, which offers rich descriptions of the interplay between human behavior and organizational structure in Congress, has many strong sociological undertones (Fenno 2003, 1978, 1973).

44. (Wingfield and Chavez 2020)

Chapter One

1. (Coffey 1978)

2. (Jones 2015)

3. (Berman 2015; Ross 2015)

4. (Brenson 2020)

5. (E. L. Scott et al. 2018)

6. (E. L. Scott et al. 2018; Brenson 2022)

7. (Rich 1974)

8. (Acker 2006, 444)

9. (Johnson 2011; King and Smith 2005; Bateman, Katznelson, and Lapinski 2018; Katznelson 2005)

10. (Holland 2007; Allen 2005)

11. (Masur 2010, 2013)

12. (King 1999, 2007)

13. (*New York Times* 1903)

14. (Jones 2023; Masur 2013)

15. The number of Black lawmakers was relatively small during this period. Reps. Oscar De Priest (1929–1935), Arthur Mitchell (1935–1943), and William Dawson (1943–1970) all represented the same majority-Black district in Chicago and served successive terms.

16. (Special Committee to Investigate the Management and Control of the House Restaurant 1934)

17. (Stainback and Tomaskovic-Devey 2012)

18. (Omi and Winant 2015)

19. (Bell 2014)

20. (Edelman 2016, 1992) The symbolic structures these organizational leaders erect are an example of what Ray (2019) identifies as racialized decoupling, delineating between the principles that supposedly guide organizational action and the active racing and gendering that shape the organization of day-to-day work. To be sure, these strategies allow racialized organizations to adapt to new racial climates rather than substantively changing in ways that might yield sustained racial progress (Seamster and Ray 2018).

21. (Barnard 1974)

22. (Russell 1974)

23. (Commission on Administrative Review 1977)

24. Lawmakers also included state and local government employees when the coverage of the Civil Rights Act extended in 1972.

25. Senator Harrison, speaking on S.2515, 92nd Cong., 2nd sess., *Congressional Record* (February 22, 1972): S 4922.

26. Senator Harrison, speaking on S.2515, 92nd Cong., 2nd sess., *Congressional Record* (February 22, 1972): S 4922.

27. (Beck 1978)

28. (Alexander 1977)

29. (Salisbury and Shepsle 1981)

30. (Beck 1978)

31. Senator Brooke, speaking on S.Res. 431, 95th Cong., 2nd sess., *Congressional Record* (October 11, 1978): S 35526.

32. ("Congress the Employer" 1984)

33. (Davies 1969; Raspberry 1969; "Congressman Serve Each Other" 1942; Beck 1978; "Waiters Walk Out on Congressman" 1942)

34. (W. Brown 1980)

35. (Eckman 2016b, 2016a)

36. (Kessler 1983a)

37. (W. Brown 1980)

38. (Kessler 1983b)

39. (Goeller 1986)

40. Representative Clay, speaking on Treatment Afforded Employees in the House of Representatives' Cafeterias is Intolerable, Unfair, and Unusual, 99th Cong., 2nd sess., *Congressional Record* 132 (March 22, 1986): 11933.

41. Representative Clay, speaking on Treatment Afforded Employees in the House of Representatives' Cafeterias Is Intolerable, Unfair, and Unusual, 99th Cong., 2nd sess., *Congressional Record* 132 (March 22, 1986): 11935.

42. (Evans 1985)

43. Representative Frank, speaking on Treatment Afforded Employees in the House of Representatives' Cafeterias Is Intolerable, Unfair, and Unusual, 99th Cong., 2nd sess., *Congressional Record* 132 (March 22, 1986): 11938.

44. Representative Frank, speaking on Treatment Afforded Employees in the House of Representatives' Cafeterias Is Intolerable, Unfair, and Unusual, 99th Cong., 2nd sess., *Congressional Record* 132 (March 22, 1986): 11936.

45. Representative Frank, speaking on Treatment Afforded Employees in the House of Representatives' Cafeterias Is Intolerable, Unfair, and Unusual, 99th Cong., 2nd sess., *Congressional Record* 132 (March 22, 1986): 11938.

46. Representative Owens, speaking on Treatment Afforded Employees in the House of Representatives' Cafeterias Is Intolerable, Unfair, and Unusual, 99th Cong., 2nd sess., *Congressional Record* 132 (March 22, 1986): 11937.

47. (Wilson and Roscigno 2016)

48. Senator Grassley, speaking on S.2, 104th Cong., 1st sess., *Congressional Record* (January 5, 1995): S-441.

49. Senator Glenn, speaking on S.2, 104th Cong., 1st sess., *Congressional Record* (January 5, 1995): S-447.

50. Senator Grassley, speaking on S.2, 104th Cong., 1st sess., *Congressional Record* (January 5, 1995): S-448.

51. (Biskupic 1995)

52. In 2018, lawmakers amended the Congressional Accountability Act and renamed the Office of Compliance (OOC) as the Office of Congressional Workplace Rights (OCWR).

53. (Timothy M. LaPira, Drutman, and Kosar 2020)

54. The House Office of Diversity and Inclusion established in the 116th Congress has begun collecting workforce data themselves rather than outsourcing this important work.

55. (Grassley 1998)

56. (Lee and Viebeck 2017)

57. (Brudney 1999, 11)

58. (Lee and Viebeck 2017)

59. (Lee and Viebeck 2017)

60. (Lee and Viebeck 2017)

61. (Gale 2017)

62. (Bade 2017)

63. (Bacon 2017; Akin 2017)

64. (Lee 2017)

65. (Lee 2017)

66. ("Hill Staff Sexual Harassment Sign-on" 2017)

67. (Back 2019)

68. (Demand Progress 2020)

69. (Brudney 1999)

70. (Grassley 1998, 48)

71. (Schuman 2020a, 2020b)

72. (Vesoulis 2022)

73. (Gregorian 2023)

74. (Cochrane and Broadwater 2022)

75. (Hubbard 2022)

76. (Saksa 2022)

77. (Saksa 2023a)

78. (Saksa 2023b)

79. (Gallup 2023)

80. US Congress, Senate, Committee on Governmental Affairs, Congressional Civil Rights Bills, 101st Cong., 1st sess., 1989, 1.

81. US Congress, Senate, Committee on Governmental Affairs, Congressional Civil Rights Bills, 101st Cong., 1st sess., 1989, 4.

Chapter Two

1. ("The Bright Young Bunch" 1978)

2. (Jordan 1979)

3. (Vera and Jenab 2017)

4. (Tilly 2000)

5. (Rivera 2016)

6. (Furnas and LaPira 2020)

7. Creation of house DEI, DEI in general.

8. (Timothy M. LaPira, Drutman, and Kosar 2020)

9. (Furnas and LaPira 2020)

10. (Jones, Win, and Vera 2021; Jones 2020)

11. (Desai 2019)

12. (Perlin 2012)

13. (Desai 2018)

14. Vera and Jenab (2017) found in the House that 8 percent of Republicans and 3.6 percent of Democrats provided paid internships. In the Senate, 51 percent of Republicans and 31 percent of the Senate provided paid internships.

15. (Kane 2019)

16. (Jones, Win, and Vera 2021)

17. Congress only reports information about interns who receive direct compensation from lawmakers. That is, we do not know the exact number of internships that remain unpaid or how many interns who work on the Hill are compensated by an external organization. This lack of transparency conceals the total number of interns and makes it difficult to evaluate the effectiveness of this new paid internship program.

18. (Snyder, de Brey, and Dillow 2018)

19. US Department of Education, National Center for Education Statistics, Integrated Postsecondary Education Data System (IPEDS).

20. (Pattillo 1999; Lacy 2007; Landry 1987)

21. (Kuhn, Schularick, and Steins 2020)

22. (Sharkey 2014, 935)

23. (Gaddis 2015; Houle and Addo 2019)

24. (Petersen, Saporta, and Seidel 2000; Ibarra 1995; Castilla 2008)

25. (Granovetter 1995)

26. (Royster 2003)

27. (Pedulla and Pager 2019)

28. Political campaigns are another important pathway to working in Congress, but they were not significant among the Black staffers I interviewed. Unsurprisingly, Black professionals are underrepresented in political campaigns (Laurison 2022; Dittmar 2015).

29. (Haile 2019)

30. (Portes 1998)

31. (Ray 2019)

32. (Ball 2020)

Chapter Three

1. (Ellison 2010, 3)

2. (Adichie 2013, 273–74)

3. A version of the chapter was previously published and is reproduced here with permission. See James Jones, "Racing through the Halls of Congress: The 'Black Nod' as an Adaptive Strategy for Surviving a Raced Institution," *Du Bois Review: Social Science Research on Race* 14, no. 1 (Spring 2017): 165–87.

4. (Dyson 2001, 93)

5. (Barris, Brown, and Patel 2014)

6. (Williams 2019)

7. (Rigueur 2014; Fields 2016)

8. (Romzek and Utter 1996; Timothy M. LaPira, Drutman, and Kosar 2020)

9. (Lamont 2000)

10. Thomas Walter designed its iconic white-cast iron dome during the 1850s, when the Capitol expanded to accommodate the growing number of lawmakers. The Statue of Freedom, designed by Thomas Crawford, sits atop the dome as a powerful symbol of our federal democracy. However, it is only because of the ingenuity of Philip A. Reid, an enslaved Black laborer, that the bronze monument exists as it does (Architect of the Capitol; Walton 2005). After a payment disagreement with an Italian sculptor who was hired to reassemble the statue from its mold, Reid solved the mystery that had left others baffled and the statue in five disjointed sections. Reid labored for over year, seven days a week, and only earned $42 for his work on Sundays to assemble the Statue of Freedom. He gained manumission in 1862, a year before the statue was put on top of the Capitol (Allen 2005; Holland 2007).

11. (Lacy 2007; Swidler 1986)

12. (Goffman 1963, 92)

13. (Goffman 1963)

14. (Doyle 1968)

15. (Bonilla-Silva 2006; Miles 2022)

16. (Feagin and Sikes 1994)

17. Elijah Anderson (2022, 2015, 2011) has written extensively about how when Black men and women enter into White spaces their behaviors are policed;

their appearances and words are scrutinized; and they are subjected to racialized disrespect.

18. (Stack 1974)

19. (Jackson 2008)

20. (Anderson 1999, 2011)

21. (Lacy 2007)

22. (Dyson 2001)

23. (Robinson 2010, 224)

24. (Jackson 2008)

25. Iddo Tavory's analysis of the nodding ritual among Orthodox Jews is instructive for contemplating the racial meaning of greetings and relations more broadly. After observing nods among Orthodox Jews who donned a yarmulke, he writes, "Rather than looking at the ways identifications are 'held' in some abstract way, potentiality is revealed in interactions with others, interactions in which members tacitly come to expect they will be 'reconstituted' in specific ways" (Tavory 2010, 53).

26. (Watkins-Hayes 2009)

27. (J. C. Scott 1985)

Chapter Four

1. Congressional Civil Rights Bills, Before the Senate Committee on Governmental Affairs, 101st Congress, 33 (1989) (Jackie Parker, Chair, Senate Black Legislative Staff Caucus).

2. Hiram Revels and Blanche K. Bruce were the first two African Americans to serve in the Senate. They were appointed in 1870 and 1874, respectively.

3. Edward Brooke was the first African American popularly elected to the US Senate. He served from 1967 to 1979. After Senator Brooke lost his reelection bid for a third term, Carol Moseley Braun was the next African American elected to the Senate in 1992.

4. Congressional Civil Rights Bills, Before the Senate Committee on Governmental Affairs, 101st Congress, 33 (1989) (Jackie Parker, Chair, Senate Black Legislative Staff Caucus).

5. (Pitkin 1967)

6. Scholars analyzing roll-call votes have found that there is no difference among how Black and White lawmakers vote on racial issues, aside from party affiliation (Haynie 2001). Alternatively, other researchers found that outside of voting behavior, there is a difference in how Black lawmakers represent minority interests and interact with Black constituents compared to White lawmakers (N. E. Brown 2014; Gamble 2007; Tillery Jr. 2011; Gay 2002; Tate 2003; Minta and Brown 2014; Minta and Sinclair-Chapman 2013; Minta 2011)

7. (Minta 2011; Haynie 2001)

8. (Grose 2011, 9)

9. (Fenno 2003)

10. (Guinier 1994; Mansbridge 1999; Mansbridge 2003)

11. For additional scholarship on the importance of personal staff in providing representation on racial issues, see Canon 1999, 205–9; Dittmar 2021; Grose, Mangum, and Martin 2007.

12. Here I build up Celeste Watkins-Hayes's (2009) concept of racialized professionalism to explain how Black staffers understand and operationalize race in their work and goals.

13. (Schultz and Shapiro 1995, 36)

14. (Dittmar 2021)

15. (Congressional Hispanic Staff Association 2010)

16. (Grose 2011)

17. (Salisbury and Shepsle 1981)

18. WIC stands for the Special Supplemental Nutrition Program for Women, Infants, and Children, which provides financial assistance and nutritious foods, especially baby formula.

19. (S. M. Collins 1997, 29)

20. (Wingfield 2013)

21. (House Office of the Legislative Counsel 2023)

22. (Crenshaw et al. 1995; Bracey 2015)

23. (Melaku 2019; Moore 2008; Pierce 2003)

24. (Moore 2008, 54)

Chapter Five

1. During this time, according to the 2010 House Compensation Study, a legislative assistant earned an average salary of $48,762 and stayed in the role for 3.1 years compared to a senior legislative assistant, who earns on average $63,508 annually and stays in the role for 3.8 years (Chief Administrative Office US House of Representatives 2010, 10–12).

2. In the 2010 House Compensation Survey, House employee referrals were the most used method to recruit for staff openings followed by internal email lists (Chief Administrative Office US House of Representatives 2010, 70).

3. (Kanter 1977; Wingfield 2013)

4. (S. M. Collins 1997)

5. (C. S. Brown and Lowery 2006)

6. Prior to the article, the Senate had not released any demographic information about its workforce since 2001 (Congressional Management Foundation 2001).

7. (Congressional Hispanic Staff Association 2010)

Chapter Six

1. (Seelye and Herndon 2018)

2. (Herndon 2018)

3. (Manning 2023)

4. (Schaeffer 2023)

5. (Ewing 2019)

6. Pressley, Ayanna. 2019. (@ayannapressley). "I love this mashup but I'm re-framing it so you can get a glimpse of some of the women behind this woman. Grateful to my dedicated A team and the committee staff for the diligent preparation that went in to yesterday's hearing #inthistogether #shinetheory @RashidaTlaib @AOC." Twitter, February 28, 2019, 10:51 p.m. https://twitter.com/ayannapressley/status/1101329146830094341?s=61&t=OizoVp-60Y0OhxACSju1Dg.

7. Pressley, Ayanna. 2020. (@ayannapressley). "This #BlackHistoryMonth I'm uplifting the critical history making role of staffers. 1st up my Staff Assistant Errin. Born & raised in Dorchester she makes the #MA7 so proud. She interned in my Council office yrs ago & its an honor to bear witness to her deliberate hard work in DC." Twitter, February 28, 2020, 11:51 a.m. https://twitter.com/ayannapressley/status/1233900606991085568?s=61&t=Wm4vMf9U42FxjTt-ZvLWBw.

8. (Biskupic 1995)

9. (Grose, Mangum, and Martin 2007)

10. (Furnas and LaPira 2020; Timothy M. LaPira 2017)

11. (Fox and Hammond 1975)

12. In a 1987 Senate hearing on applying civil rights laws to Congress, John McCain testified, "Mr. Chairman, I think this hearing is a vital step toward ending a double standard of inappropriate Congressional privilege and ending Congress's stubborn insistence on being the 'last plantation.' I don't think this double standard that exists is any more defensible than apartheid. We cannot continue to support maintaining one set of rules of privilege for ourselves and a set of far more restrictive rules for the remaining majority of society." US Congress, Senate, Committee on Governmental Affairs, Congressional Civil Rights Bills, 101st Cong., 1st sess., 1989, 5.

13. Representative De Priest, on March 21, 1934, 73rd Cong., 2nd sess., *Congressional Record* 78, pt. 5:5047.

14. (Charles W. Mills 1997)

15. (Hallett, Shulman, and Fine 2009)

16. (Tyson 2016)

17. (Page 2008)

18. (Timothy M. LaPira, Drutman, and Kosar 2020)

19. (Peterson 2020, 2021)

20. (Tillet 2012)

21. (P. H. Collins 1993)

REFERENCES

Acker, Joan. 2006. "Inequality Regimes: Gender, Class, and Race in Organizations." *Gender & Society* 20 (4): 441–64.

Adichie, Chimamanda Ngozi. 2013. *Americanah: A Novel*. New York: Alfred A. Knopf.

Akin, Stephanie. 2017. "Congress Took Three Decades to Come This Far, Sexual Harassment Victim Says." *Roll Call*, November 11. https://rollcall.com/2017/11/11/congress-took-three-decades-to-come-this-far-sexual-harassment-victim-says/.

Alexander, Andrew. 1977. "Discrimination in Hiring and Pay Starts at the Top . . . on Capitol Hill." *The Miami News*, July 14.

Allen, William C. 2005. *History of Slave Laborers in the Construction of the United States Capitol*. The Architect of the Capitol (Washington, DC). http://artandhistory.house.gov/art_artifacts/slave_labor_reportl.pdf.

Anderson, Elijah. 1999. *Code of the Street: Decency, Violence, and the Moral Life of the Inner City*. New York: W. W. Norton.

———. 2011. *The Cosmopolitan Canopy: Race and Civility in Everyday Life*. New York: W. W. Norton.

———. 2015. "The White Space." *Sociology of Race and Ethnicity* 1 (1): 10–21.

———. 2022. *Black in White Space: The Enduring Impact of Color in Everyday Life*. Chicago: The University of Chicago Press.

Architect of the Capitol. "Philip Reid and the Statue of Freedom." Accessed September 23, 2013. http://www.aoc.gov/philip-reid-and-statue-freedom.

Back, Christine J. 2019. *The Congressional Accountability Act of 1995 Reform Act: An Overview*. Congressional Research Service (Washington, DC). https://www.everycrsreport.com/files/2019-12-11_LSB10384_c6e244d089ee79daf e85148d761c445ec17b403f.pdf.

Bacon, Erin. 2017. "Predatory Behavior: The Dark Side of Capitol Hill." *Roll Call*. https://rollcall.com/2017/02/02/predatory-behavior-the-dark-side-of-capitol-hill/.

Ball, Molly. 2020. *Pelosi*. New York: Henry Holt and Company.

Barnard, Francie. 1974. "20 Hill Offices Discriminate in Hiring: 20 Congressional Offices Filed Discriminatory Job Orders." *Washington Post*, August 18.

Barris, Kenya, Njeri Brown, and Devanshi Patel. 2014. "The Nod," an episode from season 1 of the TV program "Black-ish."

Bartels, Larry M. 2009. *Unequal Democracy: The Political Economy of the New Gilded Age*. Princeton, NJ: Princeton University Press.

Bateman, David A., Ira Katznelson, and John S. Lapinski. 2018. *Southern Nation: Congress and White Supremacy after Reconstruction*. New York: Russell Sage Foundation; Princeton University Press.

Beck, Allison. 1978. "The Last Plantation: Will Employment Reform Come to Capitol Hill." *Catholic University Law Review* 28: 271–311.

Berman, Russell. 2015. "The U.S Senate Is Still One of the World's Whitest Workplaces." *The Atlantic*, December 8. http://www.theatlantic.com/politics /archive/2015/12/the-us-senate-still-one-of-the-worlds-whitest-workplaces /407488/.

Biskupic, Joan. 1995. "Judiciary Called 'Second-to-Last Plantation': With Passage of Accountability Act, Courts Are Only Branch Not Covered by Major Labor Laws." *Washington Post*, February 13.

Bonilla-Silva, Eduardo. 1997. "Rethinking Racism: Toward a Structural Interpretation." *American Sociological Review* 62 (3): 465–80. http://www.jstor .org/stable/2657316.

———. 2006. *Racism without Racists: Color-blind Racism and the Persistence of Racial Inequality in the United States*. Lanham, MD: Rowman & Littlefield Publishers.

Bourdieu, Pierre. 1984. *Distinction: A Social Critique of the Judgement of Taste*. Cambridge, MA: Harvard University Press.

Bracey, Glenn E. 2015. "Toward a Critical Race Theory of State." *Critical Sociology* 41 (3): 553–72.

Brenson, LaShonda. 2020. *Racial Diversity among Top Staff in Senate Personal Offices*. Joint Center for Political and Economic Studies (Washington, DC). https://jointcenter.org/wp-content/uploads/2020/08/2020-Senate-Report -Draft__08-21-20-5AM.pdf.

———. 2022. *Racial Diversity among Top Staff in the US House of Representatives*. The Joint Center for Political and Economic Studies (Washington, DC). https://jointcenter.org/wp-content/uploads/2022/10/Racial-Diversity -Among-Top-Staff-in-the-U.S-House-of-Representatives.pdf.

"The Bright Young Bunch." 1978. *Ebony*, May, 106–11.

Brown, C. Stone, and Mark Lowery. 2006. "Who Is Worst for Diversity? The United States Senate." *DiversityInc*, June, 170–80.

Brown, Luther. 1989. "The Last Plantation?" *Black Enterprise*, February 19.

Brown, Nadia E. 2014. *Sisters in the Statehouse: Black Women and Legislative Decision Making*. Oxford: Oxford University Press.

Brown, Warren. 1980. "Senate's Restaurant Workers Organize to Fight for Union Rights." *Washington Post*, October 10.

Brudney, James J. 1999. "Congressional Accountability and Denial: Speech or Debate Clause and Conflict of Interest Challenges to Unionization of Congressional Employees." *Harvard Journal on Legislation* 36: 1.

Burgat, Casey. 2020. "Dual Experiences—Tenure and Networks in the House of Representatives." *Congress & the Presidency* 47 (3): 338–64.

Cain, Bruce E., and Lee Drutman. 2014. "Congressional Staff and the Revolving Door: The Impact of Regulatory Change." *Election Law Journal* 13 (1): 27–44.

Canon, David T. 1999. *Race, Redistricting, and Representation: The Unintended Consequences of Black Majority Districts*. Chicago: University of Chicago Press.

Carnes, Nicholas. 2013. *White-Collar Government: The Hidden Role of Class in Economic Policy Making.* Chicago: University of Chicago Press.

Carter, Prudence L. 2003. "'Black' Cultural Capital, Status Positioning, and Schooling Conflicts for Low-Income African American Youth." *Social Problems* 50 (1): 136–55.

Castilla, E. J. 2008. "Gender, Race, and Meritocracy in Organizational Careers." *American Journal of Sociology* 113 (6): 1479–1526.

Chetty, Raj, Nathaniel Hendren, Maggie R. Jones, and Sonya R. Porter. 2019. "Race and Economic Opportunity in the United States: An Intergenerational Perspective." *The Quarterly Journal of Economics* 135 (2): 711–83. https://doi.org/10.1093/qje/qjz042. https://doi.org/10.1093/qje/qjz042.

Chief Administrative Office US House of Representatives. 2010. *2010 House Compensation Study: Guide for the 112th Congress.*

Cochrane, Emily, and Luke Broadwater. 2022. "House Votes to Extend Union Organizing Protections to Its Staff." *New York Times,* May 10. https://www.nytimes.com/2022/05/10/us/politics/house-staff-union.html.

Coffey, Raymond. 1978. "Congress Exempt from Many of Its Own Laws." *Chicago Tribune,* May 14.

Collins, Patricia Hill. 1993. "Toward a New Vision: Race, Class, and Gender as Categories of Analysis and Connection." *Race, Sex & Class* 1 (1): 25–45.

Collins, Sharon M. 1997. *Black Corporate Executives: The Making and Breaking of a Black Middle Class.* Philadelphia: Temple University Press.

Commission on Administrative Review. 1977. Administrative Review and Legislative Reorganization, Washington, DC.

"Congress the Employer." 1984. *Washington Post,* November 28.

Congressional Hispanic Staff Association. 2010. *Unrepresented: A Blueprint for Solving the Diversity Crisis on Capitol Hill.* http://media.washingtonpost.com/wp-srv/politics/documents/diversity_on_the_hill_report.pdf.

Congressional Management Foundation. 2001. *2001 Senate Staff Employment Study.* Congressional Management Foundation (Washington, DC).

"Congressman Serve Each Other." 1942. *Washington Post* June 17.

Crenshaw, Kimberle. 1990. "Mapping the Margins: Intersectionality, Identity Politics, and Violence against Women of Color." *Stanford Law Review* 43 (6): 1241.

Crenshaw, Kimberle, Neil Gotanda, Gary Peller, and Kendall Thomas, eds. 1995. *Critical Race Rheory: The Key Writings That Formed the Movement.* New York: The New Press.

Davies, George. 1969. "Hill Cafeteria Workers Strike 2 Hours." *Washington Post.*

Deering, Christopher J., and Steven S. Smith. 1997. *Committees in Congress.* 3rd ed. Washington, DC: CQ Press.

Demand Progress. 2020. "A Brief Recent History of Unionization in Congress." Accessed May 12. https://demandprogress.org/a-brief-recent-history-of-unionization-in-congress/.

Derenoncourt, Ellora, Chi Hyun Kim, Moritz Kuhn, and Moritz Schularick. 2022. *Wealth of Two Nations: The US Racial Wealth Gap, 1860–2020.* National Bureau of Economic Research.

Desai, Saahil. 2018. "When Congress Paid Its Interns." *Washington Monthly*, January 7. https://washingtonmonthly.com/2018/01/07/when-congress-paid-its-interns/.

———. 2019. "How Congress Came to Pay Its Interns." *Washington Monthly*, November 3. https://washingtonmonthly.com/2019/11/03/how-congress-came-to-pay-its-interns/.

Dittmar, Kelly. 2015. *Navigating Gendered Terrain: Stereotypes and Strategy in Political Campaigns*. Philadelphia: Temple University Press.

———. 2021. "Invisible Forces: Gender, Race, and Congressional Staff." *Politics, Groups, and Identities* 11 (1): 1–17.

Doyle, Bertram Wilbur. 1968. *The Etiquette of Race Relations in the South: A Study in Social Sontrol*. Port Washington, NY: Kennikat Press.

Du Bois, W.E.B., and Isabel Eaton. 1899. *The Philadelphia Negro: A Social Study*. Vol. 14. Publications of the University of Pennsylvania Series in Political Economy and Public Law. Philadelphia: Published for the university.

Dunnigan, Alice. 1949a. "Second Negro Named to Guard Duty in DC." *Atlanta Daily World* August 2.

———. 1949b. "A Visit to the Nation's Capitol." *Service*, December 11–16.

———. 1950. "A Visit to the Nation's Capitol." *Service*, January, 17–21.

Dyson, Michael. 2001. "Brother, Can You Spare a Nod?" *Savoy*, March.

Eckman, Sarah J. 2016a. *History of House and Senate Restaurants: Contexts for Current Operations and Issues*. Congressional Research Service (Washington, DC).

———. 2016b. *House and Senate Restaurants: Current Operations and Issues for Congress*. Congressional Research Service (Washington, DC).

Edelman, Lauren B. 1992. "Legal Ambiguity and Symbolic Structures: Organizational Mediation of Civil Rights Law." *American Journal of Sociology* 97 (6): 1531–76.

———. 2016. *Working Law: Courts, Corporations, and Symbolic Civil Rights*. Chicago: University of Chicago Press.

Ellison, Ralph. 2010. *Invisible Man*. New York: Random House. First published 1952.

Evans, Sandra. 1985. "O'Neill Supports Right to Unionize on Hill." *Washington Post*, January 04.

Ewing, Philip. 2019. "Michael Cohen Calls Trump a 'Racist' and a 'Con Man' in Scathing Testimony." NPR, February. https://www.npr.org/2019/02/27/696752450/michael-cohen-to-testify-publicly-before-congress-on-alleged-trump-lawbreaking.

Feagin, Joe R., and Melvin P. Sikes. 1994. *Living with Racism: The Black Middle-Class Experience*. Boston: Beacon Press.

Fenno, Richard F. 1973. *Congressmen in Committees*. 1st ed. Boston: Little, Brown and Company.

———. 1978. *Home Style: House Members in Their Districts*. New York: HarperCollins.

———. 2003. *Going Home: Black Representatives and Their Constituents*. Chicago: University of Chicago Press.

Fields, Corey. 2016. *Black Elephants in the Room: The Unexpected Politics of African American Republicans.* Oakland: University of California Press.

Fox, Harrison W., and Susan Webb Hammond. 1975. "The Growth of Congressional Staffs." *Proceedings of the Academy of Political Science* 32 (1): 112–24.

Fox, Harrison W., and Susan Webb Hammond. 1977. *Congressional Staffs: The Invisible Force in American Lawmaking.* New York: The Free Press.

Furnas, Alexander C., and Timothy M. LaPira. 2020. *Congressional Brain Drain: Legislative Capacity in the 21st Century.* New America Foundation (Washington DC), September 8. https://www.newamerica.org/political-reform/reports/congressional-brain-drain/.

Gaddis, S. Michael. 2015. "Discrimination in the Credential Society: An Audit Study of Race and College Selectivity in the Labor Market." *Social Forces* 93 (4): 1451–79.

Gale, Rebecca. 2017. "Where Is the Toughest Place to Report Sexual Harassment? It Might Be Capitol Hill." *Slate*, November 2. https://slate.com/human-interest/2017/11/where-is-the-toughest-place-to-report-sexual-harassment-it-might-be-capitol-hill.html.

Gallup. 2023. Congress and the Public.

Gamble, Katrina L. 2007. "Black Political Representation: An Examination of Legislative Activity within US House Committees." *Legislative Studies Quarterly* 32 (3): 421–47.

Gay, Claudine. 2002. "Spirals of Trust? The Effect of Descriptive Representation on the Relationship between Citizens and Their Government." *American Journal of Political Science* 46 (4): 717–32.

Goeller, David. 1986. "Private Meal Ticket for the House: Workers Lose Raise in Transition to Restaurant Contractor." *Washington Post* December 30.

Goffman, Erving. 1963. *Behavior in Public Places: Notes on the Social Organization of Gatherings.* New York: Free Press of Glencoe.

Gowayed, Heba. 2022. *Refuge: How the State Shapes Human Potential.* Princeton, NJ: Princeton University Press.

Granovetter, Mark S. 1995. *Getting a Job: A Study of Contacts and Careers.* 2nd ed. Chicago: University of Chicago Press.

Grassley, Charles Schmidt, and Jennifer Shaw. 1998. "Practicing What We Preach: A Legislative History of Congressional Accountability Policy Essay." *Harvard Journal on Legislation* 35: 33.

Gregorian, Dareh. 2023. "Pelosi to Offer 'Full Support' if Congressional Staffers Decide to Unionize." NBC News. Last Modified February 3, 2022. https://www.nbcnews.com/politics/congress/pelosi-offer-full-support-congressional-staff-decide-unionize-rcna14819.

Grose, Christian R. 2011. *Congress in Black and White: Race and Representation in Washington and at Home.* Cambridge; New York: Cambridge University Press.

Grose, Christian R., Maruice Mangum, and Christopher Martin. 2007. "Race, Political Empowerment, and Constituency Service: Descriptive

Representation and the Hiring of African-American Congressional Staff."
Polity 39 (4): 449–78. https://doi.org/10.1057/palgrave.polity.2300081.

Grundy, Saida. 2022. *Respectable: Politics and Paradox in Making the Morehouse Man.* Oakland: University of California Press,.

Guinier, Lani. 1994. *The Tyranny of the Majority: Fundamental Fairness in Representative Democracy.* New York: Free Press New York.

Haile, Shanelle Chambers. 2019. "Professionals, Policy Entrepreneurs, and Politicos: Congressional Staff Organizations as Career Socialization Mechanisms." Masters of Arts thesis, Department of Sociology, Brown University.

Hallett, Tim, David Shulman, and Gary Alan Fine. 2009. "Peopling Organizations: The Promise of Classic Symbolic Interactionism for an Inhabited Institutionalism." In *The Oxford Handbook of Sociology and Organization Studies: Classical Foundations,* edited by Paul Adler. Oxford: Oxford University Press.

Haynie, Kerry Lee. 2001. *African American Legislators in the American States.* New York: Columbia University Press.

Herndon, Astead W. 2018. "The Districts Are Mostly White. The Candidates Are Not." *New York Times,* July 19. https://www.nytimes.com/2018/07/19/us/politics/minority-candidates.html.

Hill Collins, Patricia. 2009. *Black Feminist Thought: Knowledge, Consciousness, and the Politics of Empowerment.* 2nd ed. New York: Routledge.

"Hill Staff Sexual Harassment Sign-on." 2017. https://docs.google.com/document/d/1h7aDKmUnDFH_48Tzg5w4viYEUTWzuFL2ukx1ksg6UaQ/edit.

Holland, Jesse J. 2007. *Black Men Built the Capitol: Discovering African-American History in and around Washington, DC.* 1st ed. Guilford, CT: Globe Pequot Press.

Houle, Jason N., and Fenaba R. Addo. 2019. "Racial Disparities in Student Debt and the Reproduction of the Fragile Black Middle Class." *Sociology of Race and Ethnicity* 5 (4): 562–77.

House Office of the Legislative Counsel. 2023. "House Office of the Legislative Counsel." Accessed June 3. https://legcounsel.house.gov.

Hubbard, Halisia. 2022. "This Congressional Staff Cecame the first in US History to Form a Union." NPR, September 27. https://www.npr.org/2022/09/27/1125257131/congress-staff-union-election-win-andy-levin.

Hunter, Marcus Anthony. 2018. *The New Black Sociologists: Historical and Contemporary Perspectives.* New York: Routledge.

Hunter, Marcus Anthony, and Zandria F. Robinson. 2018. *Chocolate Cities: The Black Map of American Life.* Oakland: University of California Press.

Ibarra, Herminia. 1995. "Race, Opportunity, and Diversity of Social Circles in Managerial Networks." *Academy of Management Journal* 38 (3): 673–703.

Jackson, John L. 2008. *Racial Paranoia: The Unintended Consequences of Political Correctness.* New York: Basic Civitas.

Johnson, Kimberley S. 2011. "Racial Orders, Congress, and the Agricultural Welfare State, 1865–1940." *Studies in American Political Development* 25 (2): 143–61.

———. 2016. "The Color Line and the State: Race and American Political Development." In *The Oxford Handbook of American Political Development,* edited by Richard Valelly, Suzanne Mettler, and Robert Lieberman. Oxford, UK: Oxford University Press.

Jones, James R. 2015. *Racial Diversity among Top Senate Staff.* Joint Center for Political and Economic Studies. https://jointcenter.org/research/racial-diversity-among-top-senate-staff.

———. 2019. "Theorizing a Racialized Congressional Workplace." In *Race, Organizations, and the Organizing Process,* edited by Melissa Wooten. Bingley, UK: Emerald Publishing Limited.

———. 2020. *The Color of Congress: Racial Representation among Interns in the US House of Representatives.* Pay Our Interns (Washington, DC). https://payourinterns.org/wp-content/uploads/2020/07/Color-Of-Congress-Report.pdf.

Jones, James R., Tiffany Win, and Carlos Mark Vera. 2021. *Who Congress Pays: Analysis of Lawmakers' Use of Intern Allowances in the 116th Congress.* Pay Our Interns https://payourinterns.org/wp-content/uploads/2021/03/Pay-Our-Interns-Who-Congress-Pays.pdf.

Jordan, Vernon. 1979. "Governments Fight Job Bias, but Practice It." *Los Angeles Times,* September 14.

Kane, Paul. 2019. "Paid Internships Are a Reality Again in Congress after Public Shaming." *Washington Post,* March 12. Accessed June 18, 2020. https://www.washingtonpost.com/politics/paid-internships-are-a-reality-again-in-congress-after-public-shaming/2019/03/12/ff371f54-44e9-11e9-94ab-d2dda3c0df52_story.html.

Kanter, Rosabeth Moss. 1977. *Men and Women of the Corporation.* New York: Basic Books.

Katznelson, Ira. 2005. *When Affirmative Action Was White: An Untold History of Racial Inequality in Twentieth-Century America.* New York: W. W. Norton & Company.

Kessler, Ronald. 1983a. "Congress' Cafeteria Workers Enlist UN in Labor Battle." *Washington Post,* May 30, 1983a.

———. 1983b. "Employees of Senate Cafeterias Vote against Being Represented by Union." *Washington Post,* September 15, 1983b.

King, Desmond S. 1999. "The Racial Bureaucracy: African Americans and the Federal Government in the Era of Segregated Race Relations." *Governance* 12 (4): 345–77.

———. 2007. *Separate and Unequal: African Americans and the US Federal Government.* Rev. ed. Oxford; New York: Oxford University Press.

King, Desmond S., and Rogers M. Smith. 2005. "Racial Orders in American Political Development." *American Political Science Review* 99 (1): 75–92.

Kofmehl, Kenneth T. 1977. *Professional Staffs of Congress.* West Lafayette, IL: Purdue University Press.

Kuhn, Moritz, Moritz Schularick, and Ulrike I. Steins. 2020. "Income and Wealth Inequality in America, 1949–2016." *Journal of Political Economy* 128 (9): 3469–3519. https://doi.org/10.1086/708815.

Lacy, Karyn R. 2007. *Blue-Chip Black: Race, Class, and Status in the New Black Middle Class.* Berkeley: University of California Press.

Lamont, Michèle. 2000. *The Dignity of Working Men: Morality and the Boundaries of Race, Class, and Immigration*. New York; Cambridge, MA: Russell Sage Foundation; Harvard University Press.

Landry, Bart. 1987. *The New Black Middle Class*. Oakland: University of California Press.

LaPira, Timothy M., Lee Drutman, and Kevin R. Kosar. 2020. *Congress Overwhelmed: The Decline in Congressional Capacity and Prospects for Reform*. Chicago: University of Chicago Press.

LaPira, Timothy M. 2017. *Revolving Door Lobbying: Public Service, Private Influence, and the Unequal Representation of Interests*. Lawrence: University Press of Kansas.

Laurison, Daniel. 2022. *Producing Politics: Inside the Exclusive Campaign World Where the Privileged Few Shape Politics for All of Us*. Boston: Beacon Press.

Lee, Michelle Ye Hee. 2017. "This Congresswoman Is Starting #MeTooCongress to Draw Attention to Sexual Harassment on Capitol Hill." *Washington Post*, October 27. https://www.washingtonpost.com/news/powerpost/wp/2017/10/27/this-congresswoman-is-starting-metoocongress-to-draw-attention-to-sexual-harassment-on-capitol-hill/.

Lee, Michelle Ye Hee, and Elise Viebeck. 2017. "Treasury Paid $174,000 in Taxpayer Money to Settle House Sexual Harassment Claims." *Washington Post*, December 19. https://www.washingtonpost.com/powerpost/new-data-released-on-house-harassment-sex-discrimination-claim-settlements/2017/12/19/472f49d6-e4c8-11e7-833f-155031558ff4_story.html.

Lieberman, Robert C. 2001. *Shifting the Color Line: Race and the American Welfare State*. Cambridge, MA: Harvard University Press.

Malbin, Michael J. 1980. *Unelected Representatives: Congressional Staff and the Future of Representative Government*. New York: Basic Books.

Mann, Robert. 2007. *When Freedom Would Triumph: The Civil Rights Struggle in Congress, 1954–1968*. Baton Rouge: Louisiana State University Press.

Manning, Jennifer E. 2023. *Membership of the 118th Congress: A Profile*. Congressional Research Service (Washington, DC). https://crsreports.congress.gov/product/pdf/R/R47470.

Mansbridge, Jane. 1999. "Should Blacks Represent Blacks and Women Represent Women? A Contingent 'Yes.'" *The Journal of Politics* 61 (3): 628–57.

———. 2003. "Rethinking Representation." *American Political Science Review* 97 (4): 515–28.

Masur, Kate. 2010. *An Example for All the Land: Emancipation and the Struggle over Equality in Washington, DC*. Chapel Hill: University of North Carolina Press.

———. 2013. "Patronage and Protest in Kate Brown's Washington." *Journal of American History* 99 (4): 1047–71.

Mayhew, David. 1974. *Congress: The Electoral Connection*. New Haven, CT: Yale University Press.

McCrain, Joshua. 2018. "Revolving Door Lobbyists and the Value of Congressional Staff Connections." *The Journal of Politics* 80 (4): 1369–83.

Melaku, Tsedale M. 2019. *You Don't Look Like a Lawyer: Black Women and Systemic Gendered Racism.* Lanham, MD: Rowman & Littlefield.

Miles, Corey J. 2022. "Sociology of Vibe: Blackness, Felt Criminality, and Emotional Epistemology." *Humanity & Society* 43 (3): 365–84. https://doi.org /https://doi.org/10.1177/01605976221146733.

Mills, C. Wright. 2000. *The Power Elite.* Oxford: Oxford University Press.

Mills, Charles W. 1997. *The Racial Contract.* Ithaca, NY: Cornell University Press.

Minta, Michael D. 2011. *Oversight: Representing the Interests of Blacks and Latinos in Congress.* Princeton, NJ: Princeton University Press.

Minta, Michael D., and Nadia E. Brown. 2014. "Interesecting Interests: Gender, Race, and Congressional Attention to Women's Issues." *Du Bois Review: Social Science Research on Race* 11 (2): 253–72. https://doi.org/10.1017 /S1742058X14000186. https://www.cambridge.org/core/article/intersecting -interests/5DAE336A79593AD1B76EA2A73D10D2FB.

Minta, Michael D., and Valeria Sinclair-Chapman. 2013. "Diversity in Political Institutions and Congressional Responsiveness to Minority iIterests." *Political Research Quarterly* 66 (1): 127–40.

Montgomery, Jacob M., and Brendan Nyhan. 2017. "The Effects of Congressional Staff Networks in the US House of Representatives." *The Journal of Politics* 79 (3): 745–61.

Moore, Wendy Leo. 2008. *Reproducing Racism: White Space, Elite Law Schools, and Racial Inequality.* Lanham, MD: Rowman & Littlefield Publishers.

Murakawa, Naomi. 2014. *The First Civil Right: How Liberals Built Prison America.* Oxford: Oxford University Press.

Nelson, Alondra. 2016. *The Social life of DNA: Race, Reparations, and Reconciliation after the Genome.* Boston: Beacon Press.

New York Times. 1903. "Noted Negro Is Dead." November 17.

Nkomo, Stella M. 1992. "The Emperor Has No Clothes: Rewriting 'Race in Organizations.'" *Academy of Management Review* 17 (3): 487–513.

North, James. 1978. "Congress: The Last Plantation." *Barrister* 5 (50): 46–56.

Office of the Historian, United States House of Representatives. 2023. "Black Americans in Congress." Accessed June 1. https://history.house.gov/baic/.

Oliver, Melvin, and Thomas Shapiro. 2013. *Black Wealth/White Wealth: A New Perspective on Racial Inequality.* New York: Routledge.

Omi, Michael, and Howard Winant. 2015. *Racial Formation in the United States.* 3rd ed. New York: Routledge/Taylor & Francis Group.

Page, Scott E. 2008. *The Difference: How the Power of Diversity Creates Better Groups, Firms, Schools, and Societies.* Princeton, NJ: Princeton University Press.

Pattillo, Mary E. 1999. *Black Picket Fences: Privilege and Peril among the Black Middle Class.* Chicago: University of Chicago Press.

Pedulla, David S., and Devah Pager. 2019. "Race and Networks in the Job Search Process." *American Sociological Review* 84 (6): 983–1012.

Perlin, Ross. 2012. *Intern Nation: How to Earn Nothing and Learn Little in the Brave New Economy.* New York: Verso Books.

Petersen, T., I. Saporta, and M.D.L. Seidel. 2000. "Offering a Job: Meritocracy and Social Networks." *American Journal of Sociology* 106 (3): 763–816.

Peterson, R. Eric. 2020. *Senate Staff Levels in Member, Committee, Leadership, and Other Offices, 1977–2020.* Congressional Research Service (Washington, DC). https://sgp.fas.org/crs/misc/R43946.pdf.

———. 2021. *House of Representatives Staff Levels in Member, Committee, Leadership, and Other Offices, 1977–2021.* Congressional Research Service (Washington, DC). https://crsreports.congress.gov/product/pdf/R/R43947.

Pierce, Jennifer L. 2003. "'Racing for Innocence': Whiteness, Corporate Culture, and the Backlash against Affirmative Action." *Qualitative Sociology* 26: 53–70.

Pitkin, Hanna F. 1967. *The Concept of Representation.* Vol. 75. Oakland: University of California Press.

Portes, Alejandro. 1998. "Social Capital: Its Origins and Applications in Modern Sociology." *Annual Review of Sociology* 24 (1): 1–24.

Raspberry, William. 1969. "Plight of Hill Food Workers Reveals Recipe for a Revolt." *Washington Post.*

Ray, Victor. 2019. "A Theory of Racialized Organizations." *American Sociological Review* 84 (1): 26–53.

Rich, Spencer. 1974. "28 Blacks Have Top Senate Jobs." *Washington Post,* March 31.

Rigueur, Leah Wright. 2014. *The Loneliness of the Black Republican: Pragmatic Politics and the Pursuit of Power.* Princeton, NJ: Princeton University Press.

Ritchie, Melinda N., and Hye Young You. 2019. *Women's Advancement in Politics: Evidence from Congressional Staff.* Working Paper.

Rivera, Lauren A. 2016. *Pedigree: How Elite Students Get Elite Jobs.* Princeton, NJ: Princeton University Press.

Robinson, Eugene. 2010. *Disintegration: The Splintering of Black America.* 1st ed. New York: Doubleday.

Romzek, Barbara S. 2000. "Accountability of Congressional Staff." *Journal of Public Administration Research and Theory* 10 (2): 413–46.

Romzek, Barbara S., and Jennifer A. Utter. 1996. "Career Dynamics of Congressional Legislative Staff: Preliminary Profile and Research Questions." *Journal of Public Administration Research and Theory* 6 (3): 415–42.

———. 1997. "Congressional Legislative Staff: Political Professionals or Clerks?" *American Journal of Political Science* 41 (4): 1251–79.

Rosenthal, Cindy Simon. 2000. "Gender Styles in State Legislative Committees: Raising Their Voices and Resolving Conflict." *Women and Politics* 21 (2): 21–45.

———. 2002. *Women Transforming Congress.* Vol. 4. Norman: University of Oklahoma Press.

Rosenthal, Cindy Simon, and Lauren C. Bell. 2003. "From Passive to Active Representation: The Case of Women Congressional Staff." *Journal of Public Administration Research and Theory* 13 (1): 65–82.

Ross, Janell. 2015. "On Capitol Hill, the United States Is a Very, Very White Place." *Washington Post,* December 8. https://www.washingtonpost.com/news/the-fix/wp/2015/12/08/on-capitol-hill-the-united-states-is-a-very-very-white-place/.

Royster, Deirdre A. 2003. *Race and the Invisible Hand: How White Networks Exclude Black Men from Blue-Collar Jobs*. Berkeley: University of California Press.

Russell, Mary. 1974. "Blacks' Race Indicated on Hill Job Applications." *Washington Post*, August 24.

Saksa, Jim. 2022. "Staffers in Rep. Andy Levin's Office Sign First Union Contract." *Roll Call*, October 17. https://rollcall.com/2022/10/17/staffers-in-rep-andy -levins-office-sign-first-union-contract/.

———. 2023a. "House Republicans' Attempt to Block Staffer Unions May Have Missed Mark." *Roll Call*, March 13. https://rollcall.com/2023/03/13/house -republicans-attempt-to-block-staffer-unions-may-have-missed-mark/.

———. 2023b. "With Voluntary Recognition, Ed Markey's Staff Will Be the First in the Senate to Unionize." *Roll Call*, March 8. https://rollcall.com/2023/03 /08/with-voluntary-recognition-ed-markeys-staff-will-be-the-first-in-the -senate-to-unionize/.

Salisbury, Robert H., and Kenneth A. Shepsle. 1981. "US Congressman as Enterprise." *Legislative Studies Quarterly* 6 (4): 559–76.

Schaeffer, Katherine. 2023. "The Changing Face of Congress in 8 Charts." Pew Research Center. Last Modified February 7. Accessed May 29. https://www .pewresearch.org/short-reads/2023/02/07/the-changing-face-of-congress/.

Schultz, Craig, and Richard Shapiro. 1995. *Senate Staff Employment: 1995 Salaries, Tenure, Demographics and Benefits*. Congressional Management Foundation. https://s3.amazonaws.com/demandprogress/documents/1995 _Senate_Staff_Employment.pdf.

Schuman, Daniel. 2020a. *Recommendation for Updating the House Rules 117th Congress*. Demand Progress, September 24. https://s3.amazonaws.com /demandprogress/reports/Recommendation_for_Updating_the_House _Rules_117th_Congress.pdf.

———.2020b. *Recommendations for Strengthening the Senate 117th Congress*. Demand Progress. September 30. https://s3.amazonaws.com /demandprogress/reports/Recommendations_for_Strengthening_the _Senate_-_117th_Congress.pdf.

Scott, Elsie L., Karra W. McCray, Donald Bell, and Spencer Overton. 2018. *Racial Diversity among Top US House Staff*. Joint Center for Political and Economic Studies (Washington, DC). https://jointcenter.org/wp-content/uploads/2019 /11/Racial-Diversity-Among-Top-US-House-Staff-9-11-18-245pm-1.pdf.

Scott, James C. 1985. *Weapons of the Weak: Everyday Forms of Peasant Resistance*. New Haven, CT: Yale University Press.

Seamster, Louise, and Victor Ray. 2018. "Against Teleology in the Study of Race: Toward the Abolition of the Progress Paradigm." *Sociological Theory* 36 (4): 315–42.

Seelye, Katharine Q., and Astead W. Herndon. 2018. "Ayanna Pressley Seeks Her Political Moment in a Changing Boston." *New York Times*, September 1. https://www.nytimes.com/2018/09/01/us/politics/ayanna-pressley -massachusetts.html.

Sewell Jr., William H. 1992. "A Theory of Structure: Duality, Agency, and Trans-formation." *American Journal of Sociology* 98 (1): 1–29.

Sharkey, Patrick. 2014. "Spatial Segmentation and the Black Middle Class." *American Journal of Sociology* 119 (4): 903–54.

Shedd, Carla. 2015. *Unequal City: Race, Schools, and Perceptions of Injustice.* New York: Russell Sage Foundation.

Smith, Sandra Susan. 2005. "'Don't Put My Name on It': Social Capital Activation and Job-Finding Assistance among the Black Urban Poor." *American Journal of Sociology* 111 (1): 1–57.

Snyder, Thomas D., Cristobal de Brey, and Sally A. Dillow. 2018. *Digest of Education Statistics.* National Center for Education Statistics, Institute of Education Sciences, US Department of Education (Washington, DC).

Special Committee to Investigate the Management and Control of the House Restaurant. 1934. *Authority of Committee on Accounts, House of Representatives.* US House of Representatives.

Stack, Carol B. 1974. *All Our Kin: Strategies for Survival in a Black Community.* 1st ed. New York: Harper & Row.

Stainback, Kevin, and Donald Tomaskovic-Devey. 2012. *Documenting Desegregation: Racial and Gender Segregation in Private Sector Employment since the Civil Rights Act.* New York: Russell Sage Foundation.

Swidler, Ann. 1986. "Culture in action: Symbols and strategies." *American sociological review*: 273–286.

Tate, Katherine. 2003. *Black Faces in the Mirror: African Americans and Their Representatives in the US Congress.* Princeton, NJ: Princeton University Press.

Tavory, Iddo. 2010. "Of Yarmulkes and Categories: Delegating Boundaries and the Phenomenology of Interactional Expectation." *Theory and Society* 39 (1): 49–68.

Tillery Jr., Alvin B. 2011. *Between Homeland and Motherland: Africa, US Foreign Policy, and Black Leadership in America.* Ithaca, NY: Cornell University Press.

Tillet, Salamishah. 2012. *Sites of Slavery: Citizenship and Racial Democracy in the Post–Civil Rights Imagination.* Durham, NC: Duke University Press.

Tilly, Charles. 2000. "Relational Studies of Inequality." *Contemporary Sociology* 29 (6): 782–85.

Tomaskovic-Devey, Donald, and Dustin Robert Avent-Holt. 2019. *Relational Inequalities: An Organizational Approach.* New York: Oxford University Press.

Torres-Spelliscy, Ciara. 2017. "Time Suck: How the Fundraising Treadmill Diminishes Effective Governance." *Seton Hall Legislative Journal* 42: 271.

Traister, Rebecca. 2022. "The Institutionalist." *The Cut.*

Tyson, Vanessa C. 2016. *Twists of fate: Multiracial Coalitions and Minority Representation in the US House of Representatives.* Oxford and New York: Oxford University Press.

United States Congress, House Committee on House Administration, and United States. Congress, House Office of History and Preservation. 2008. *Black Americans in Congress, 1870–2007.* Washington, DC: US GPO.

Vera, Carlos, and Daniel Jenab. 2017. *Experience Doesn't Pay the Bills: Why Paid Internships Are a Must in Congress*. Pay Our Interns (Washington, DC). https://payourinterns.org/wp-content/uploads/2018/01/Payourinternsreport.pdf.

Vesoulis, Abby. 2022. "Inside the Capitol Hill Staffers' Effort to Unionize Congress." *Time*, March 26. https://time.com/6160944/capitol-hill-staff-union-congress/.

"Waiters Walk Out on Congressman." 1942. *New York Times* June 17.

Walton, Eugene. 2005. "Philip Reid and the Statue of Freedom." *Social Education* 69 (5): 1–16.

Watkins-Hayes, Celeste. 2009. *The New Welfare Bureaucrats: Entanglements of Race, Class, and Policy Reform*. Chicago: University of Chicago Press.

Weil, Julie Zauzmer, Adrian Blanco, and Leo Dominguez. 2022. "More than 1,800 Congressmen once Enslaved Black People. This Is Who They Were, and How They Shaped the Nation." *Washington Post*, January 10. https://www.washingtonpost.com/history/interactive/2022/congress-slaveowners-names-list/.

Williams, Anthony James. 2019. "Black in Public: How Witnessing among Strangers Subverts Surveillance on Public Transit." Unpublished manuscript.

Wilson, George, and Vincent J. Roscigno. 2016. "Neo-liberal Reform, the Public Sector and Black–White Inequality." *Sociology Compass* 10 (12): 1141–49. https://doi.org/https://doi.org/10.1111/soc4.12439.

Wingfield, Adia Harvey. 2013. *No More Invisible Man: Race and Gender in Men's Work*. Philadelphia: Temple University Press.

———. 2019. *Flatlining: Race, Work, and Health Care in the New Economy*. Oakland: University of California Press.

Wingfield, Adia Harvey, and Koji Chavez. 2020. "Getting In, Getting Hired, Getting Sideways Looks: Organizational Hierarchy and Perceptions of Racial Discrimination." *American Sociological Review* 85 (1): 31–57.

Wooten, Melissa E. 2019. *Race, Organizations, and the Organizing Process*. Bingley, UK: Emerald Group Publishing.

Wooten, Melissa E., and Lucius Couloute. 2017. "The Production of Racial Inequality within and among Organizations." *Sociology Compass* 11 (1): 1–10.

Young, Alford A. 2004. *The Minds of Marginalized Black Men: Making Sense of Mobility, Opportunity, and Future Life Chances*. Princeton, NJ: Princeton University Press.

INDEX

A NOTE ON THE TYPE

THIS BOOK has been composed in Miller, a Scotch Roman typeface designed by Matthew Carter and first released by Font Bureau in 1997. It resembles Monticello, the typeface developed for The Papers of Thomas Jefferson in the 1940s by C. H. Griffith and P. J. Conkwright and reinterpreted in digital form by Carter in 2003.

Pleasant Jefferson ("P. J.") Conkwright (1905–1986) was Typographer at Princeton University Press from 1939 to 1970. He was an acclaimed book designer and AIGA Medalist.

The ornament used throughout this book was designed by Pierre Simon Fournier (1712–1768) and was a favorite of Conkwright's, used in his design of the *Princeton University Library Chronicle*.